21
DAYS
to Your
TOTAL
HEALING

Morris Cerullo

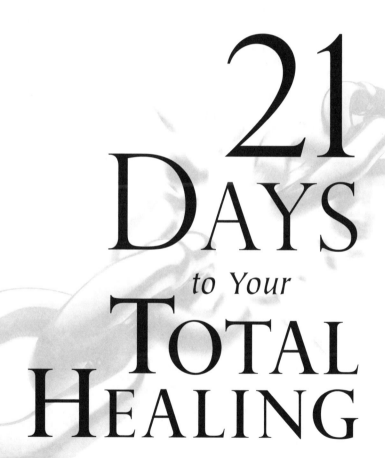

21
Days
to Your
Total
Healing

DESTINY IMAGE® PUBLISHERS, INC.

P.O. Box 310, Shippensburg, PA 17257-0310

"Speaking to the Purposes of God for This Generation and for the Generations to Come."

This book and all other Destiny Image, Revival Press, MercyPlace, Fresh Bread, Destiny Image Fiction, and Treasure House books are available at Christian bookstores and distributors worldwide.

Previously published by Morris Cerullo World Evangelism
Copyright 2009

For a U.S. bookstore nearest you, call 1-800-722-6774.

For more information on foreign distributors, call 717-532-3040.

Or reach us on the Internet: www.destinyimage.com

Trade Paper ISBN: 978-0-7684-3254-1
Hardcover ISBN: 978-0-7684-3447-7
Large Print ISBN: 978-0-7684-3448-4
Ebook ISBN: 978-0-7684-9115-9

For Worldwide Distribution, Printed in the U.S.A.

1 2 3 4 5 6 7 8 / 14 13 12 11 10

Table of Contents

Part II
God's Sevenfold Contract of Divine Healing!

Part III
Your Seven-Point Strategy to Defeat Satan's Attacks Against Your Physical Body

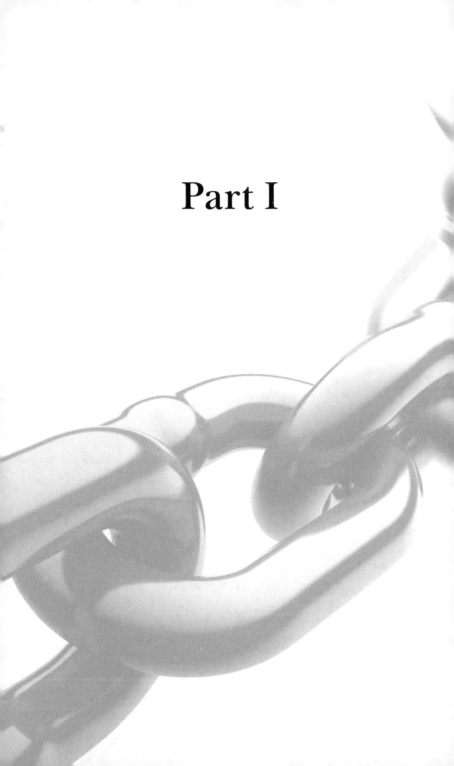

Part I

SEVEN MAJOR POINTS OF SATAN'S ATTACKS AGAINST YOUR PHYSICAL BODY

SPIRITUAL WEARINESS AND PHYSICAL EXHAUSTION

So shall My word be that goeth forth out of My mouth: it shall not return unto Me void, but it shall accomplish that which I please, and it shall prosper in the thing whereto I sent it
(Isaiah 55:11).

Scripture Reading: Mark 5:25-34

One of satan's major attacks against your physical body is to try to place a spirit of weariness upon you so that you will be totally exhausted spiritually, mentally, and physically. He wants to drain you of your physical strength and bring you to a point where you feel continually tired—worn-out! His strategy is to wear you down to the point of being so exhausted that you are *(handwritten annotation at top:)* Keep speaking Faith Filled words → Make a Demand on the goodness of God (His love) For you & therefore His anointing To heal you!

too tired to pray, study the Word, or to continue resisting his attacks on your body.

In the story of the woman who suffered with an issue of blood for 12 years, she had come to a place where she had exhausted all of her resources. She had suffered many things of her doctors and, in the natural, had come to a place where she must have been worn out mentally, as well as physically. In the natural, there was nothing left for her to do but to go home and die. That is, until she heard about Jesus, and faith began to stir within her.

She didn't give up! She pressed her way through the crowds: *"For she said, If I may touch but His clothes, I shall be whole"* (Mark 5:28). The Amplified Bible says: *"For she kept saying, If I only touch His garments, I shall be restored to health"* (Mark 5:28 AMP). As she pressed her way through to Christ, she kept speaking, "If I can touch the hem of His garments, I will be healed. If I can touch the hem of His garments, I will be healed!" As she focused her faith on Christ, acted in faith, and kept speaking faith-filled words, it made a demand on the healing anointing that was upon Jesus, and healing was manifested in her body.

Think about the sickness, pain, turmoil, emotional stress, and anxiety that satan uses in an attempt to discourage and defeat you.

→Don't stop believing for your Healing, deliverance a provision! ✗

Refuse to allow satan to wear you down spiritually and physically.

Regardless of how long you have suffered or been afflicted, don't stop believing and persevering in faith for your healing.

Jesus destroyed the works of satan. He rendered him ineffective. (1 Jn 3:8

You are set free from the things that satan may use against you.

The pain, sickness, and disease—*Poverty*—which are part of the curse that satan brings against God's children—are **illegal.** Christ became a curse and *"redeemed us from the curse of the law"* (Gal. 3:13.)

Satan's Attacks on Your Physical Body Are Illegal!

One of the major strategies in your counterattack against satan and to receive your healing is in understanding the true source and origin of sickness and disease. Make no mistake about it! Satan wants you to be sick physically! He will use every lie and strategy possible to block and hinder you from receiving your healing. His objective is to steal, kill, and destroy (see John 10:10).

It is never the will of the Father for us to be afflicted with disease and sickness. To believe that God afflicts people with sickness is to believe the lies of the devil!

God never intended for us to experience pain, sickness, disease, or death. These things entered the world through Adam's and Eve's disobedience in the Garden of Eden. As a result of their sin, humankind came under the curse and its consequences, which include sickness, disease, and death.

Pain, sorrow

God, in His great love and mercy, didn't leave humankind under the curse of sin, sickness, and death. He sent Jesus and anointed Him to destroy the works of the devil and break the curse off humankind. *"How God anointed Jesus of Nazareth with the Holy Ghost and with power: who went about doing good, and healing all that were oppressed of the devil; for God was with Him"* (Acts 10:38). He came to *"destroy the works of the devil"* (1 John 3:8)!

Satan Is a Thief, Deceiver, Liar, Murderer, and Destroyer!

Satan and his demons afflict and torment people with sicknesses and diseases. He deceives people into blaming God for their sickness and believing that it is not God's will to heal them.

Cancer, heart disease, diabetes, arthritis, multiple sclerosis, blindness, deafness, paralysis, and all other sicknesses and diseases are a result of humankind's fall and the consequences of sin. God does not send loathsome sicknesses or debilitating, crippling diseases upon His children to chastise them. It is never His will for His children to be bound by sickness, eaten up with cancer, or to suffer excruciating pain until they die. From cover-to-cover, the Word of God reveals that it is His will to heal all who come to Him in faith.

Two thousand years ago, God provided a way to set humankind free from the bondages of sin, sickness, and disease. He sent Jesus to pay the price, break those bondages, save our souls, and heal our bodies. In contrast to satan—who comes to steal, kill, and destroy—Jesus said: *"I am come that they might have life, and that they might have it more abundantly"* (John 10:10).

Satan Wants to Wear Down Your Resistance

Your CAPAbility To Resist!

Becoming spiritually weary is one of the most dangerous positions that you can be in. When you are spiritually weary, it will affect you mentally and physically. Satan will try to wear you out. Unless you are aware of what is happening, and prepare yourself for the battle, you will not be able to stand. You cannot afford to be ignorant of satan's strategies! (See Second Corinthians 2:11.)

Financial Lack!

Satan will attack you through your circumstances and will try to place sicknesses and diseases on your body. He will then bombard your mind with fear, worry, and doubt, until you become spiritually weary. At this point, if you faint in your mind, you will become discouraged, lose hope, and resign yourself to accept your sickness and your circumstances. Your discouragement will lead to depression, and depression will eventually affect your body. Once your spiritual and physical resistance is down, you will be more vulnerable to sickness, disease, and the attacks of the enemy.

God's Word Is Your Prescription for Healing

God's divine healing is spiritual. It is first received in your spirit before there is an outward manifestation of your healing. However, if your spirit is overwhelmed, and you have become spiritually weary, you will be unable to resist the attacks of the devil on your body, receive God's Word, or release your faith.

We read in Psalm 107:20: *"He sent His word, and healed them."* God's Word is supernatural. It works through the human spirit and is a spiritual cure. God's Word is alive with the power of Almighty God. Jesus said, *"The words that I speak unto you, they are spirit, and they are life"* (John 6:63).

God's Word is health (or medicine) to your flesh. (Read Proverbs 4:20-22.) Healing can be received into the human spirit through the Word. In the same way that you take medicine into your physical body to aid healing by physical means, you must also receive God's Word for healing into your spirit for supernatural healing.

The Seed for Your Miracle Is in the Word

When you speak the Word of God over your body and into your circumstances in faith, the power of God is there to manifest the healing that you need. God has said: *"So shall My word be that goeth forth out of My mouth: it shall not return unto Me void, but it shall accomplish that which I please, and it shall prosper in the thing whereto I sent it"* (Isa. 55:11). As you claim God's promises of healing, and speak them over your body, they will not return void. Praise God! They will accomplish God's purpose!

Jesus said: *"If ye abide in Me, and My words abide in you, ye shall ask what ye will, and it shall be done unto you"* (John 15:7). To counterattack satan's attacks to wear you down physically, spiritually, and mentally, the Word must abide (remain in you) so that it will take root in your spirit. This involves more than just reading the Word or even repeating Scripture. You must meditate on God's promises concerning healing, and bring your thoughts into submission to the Word until it becomes a part of you. Then, when you speak His promises by faith into your circumstances and over your body, it will result in healing!

Continually Confess God's Word Over Your Body

God's Word is medicine to your flesh and is the most powerful medicine available today. Confess His promises of healing over your body on a regular basis. The moment you feel that you are becoming fearful, worried, discouraged, depressed, or spiritually and physically worn out, recognize it as an attack of satan. Resist the thoughts that he is using against you, in the name of Jesus. Continue to claim and act in faith on His Word. Know that God's Word cannot and will not fail!

Stop speaking words of sickness, unbelief, fear, discouragement, and defeat! When you continually talk about your sickness and disease—moan, groan, and complain about your pains and speak words of fear, doubt, and unbelief—you are blocking the manifestation of God's healing power in your body.

The same mighty, resurrection power—and the same healing power that was released through Christ as He spoke healing—is in His Word! As you speak and confess God's promises of healing and deliverance, you will feel God's Spirit within you quickening you and releasing a flow of His power into your body. Paul told the Romans: *"The word is nigh thee, even in thy mouth, and in thy heart: that is, the word of faith, which we preach"* (Rom. 10:8).

Regardless of how you may feel, or the visible manifestation of symptoms of sickness and disease in your body, as you continually speak forth the Word in faith, the healing power of God will be released. It will destroy the disease in your body.

————◄o►————

Claim This Scripture Throughout the Day for Your Healing:

> *And the Lord will take away from thee all sickness, and will put none of the evil diseases of Egypt, which thou knowest, upon thee* (Deuteronomy 7:15).

————◄o►————

Make the Following Your Confession of Faith Today:

> *Knowing that God's Word will not return unto Him void but will accomplish His purposes, I reject all spiritual weariness and physical exhaustion. I*

→ WORD
→ Love
→ goodness
→ Anointing
→ power

speak life and healing to every part of my body, soul, and spirit. Jesus carried my sins and my sicknesses upon Himself. He has removed them from me. I declare that by His stripes, I am healed and made whole. God sent His Word and healed me!

- Keep Speaking "Faith Filled Words" - Don't stop! until Manifestation"
- Make A Demand on God's Word, God's Love, God's goodness, God's Anointing
- Don't stop Believing For your healing & Deliverance! & God's power
- Satan's Attacks on God's children Are Illegal" Gal. 3:13
- Your prescription For your healing is Declaring God's Word
      Deliverance   Through your Trial!
      Guidance
      Provision

↳ How else Are we to Face "our circumstances"? Passively? worried?, Non-caringly? & Axious? Indifferntly? Troubled?

→ The Benefits of Above must "First" Be Believed & Received
  IN OUR SPIRITS!, Before They will Manifest physically!
  (In the mean Time → be Faithful, believing, obedient, submissive To God
  And Serve Him By Mat 6:33"

CAUSING YOU TO KEEP YOUR EYES
FOCUSED ON YOUR
PAIN AND SYMPTOMS

Things hoped For!
The evidence of
Things not seen!

Now faith is the substance of things hoped for, the evidence of things not seen (Hebrews 11:1).

Scripture Reading: Second Kings 4:18-37

When the Shunnamite woman's son died, she refused to focus on the obvious natural symptoms showing that he was dead. When they brought him to her, she held him on her lap until he died. When she realized that he was dead, she did not call for her husband and the mourners or accept the fact that he was dead. She carried his lifeless body, laid him on the bed, and shut the door.

Instead of giving in to despair, she acted in faith and went to get the prophet of God. She believed that God would heal her son. She believed that the same God who healed her barren womb and enabled her to give birth to her son was able to breathe life into him and resurrect him from the dead.

Her focus wasn't on the lifeless body of her son lying on the bed. Her eyes were focused on the almighty power of the God of Elisha. Instead of weeping and crying words of fear and unbelief, she spoke words of faith. She told her husband: *"It shall be well"* (2 Kings 4:23).

When Elisha saw her coming, he sent Gehazi to ask her if all was well. Again, the woman did not speak words of doubt and fear, but said: *"It is well"* (2 Kings 4:26). The woman received her son back from the dead because she refused to keep her eyes focused on the outward symptoms of her son's physical condition. She persevered in faith until she received a miracle!

Refuse to React According to Your Feelings or Symptoms

Satan's strategy is to cause you to become so overwhelmed by your symptoms, pain, the doctor's prognosis, and the condition of your body that you cannot see beyond them. When he attacks your physical body with sickness, he wants you to react according to what you see in the natural, according to your natural senses, instead of looking beyond your sickness, beyond your pain and the symptoms, to an all-powerful God who has provided healing and deliverance for you.

Satan wants you to rely on your feelings instead of trusting and acting on God's Word.

The devil will tell you, "You can't claim your healing. You are not healed—just look at your symptoms. Your pain isn't gone. You couldn't possibly be healed." You must refuse to listen to the devil, reject the negative forces of unbelief, and believe God for your healing. Be fully persuaded that God is faithful and will do all He has promised.

As long as you keep your eyes on your physical condition, your faith will waver. This will cause you to question God and doubt His will to heal you. If your faith wavers, you will not be able to receive your healing.

In the book, *Smith Wigglesworth on Healing*, Wigglesworth says:

> *You will never get anywhere if you depend on your feelings. There is something a thousand times better than feelings, and it is the powerful Word of God. There is a divine revelation within you*

that came when you were born from above, and this is real faith. "Oh, beloved, may God help us to get our eyes off the conditions and symptoms, no matter how bad they may be, and get them fastened on Him."[1]

Act in Faith, Regardless of Natural Circumstances

To act in faith on God's promises for your healing, you must not be governed by your natural senses. Feeling, smelling, tasting, hearing, and seeing are the senses by which the natural man is directed. However, the two factors by which the spiritual man is directed are God's Word and faith. You must receive your healing by faith, regardless of the symptoms of your sickness or disease and regardless of your feelings.

In his book, *Healing the Sick,* T.L. Osborn (writing on faith that acts, regardless of natural circumstances) states:

Genuine faith in God and in His Word is stepping out upon what He has said, regardless of what one sees or feels or senses in the natural. Faith is a decisive act, depending only upon God's Word. Faith ignores every natural symptom or evidence which is contrary to what God's Word states.[2]

Never be afraid to act on God's Word because there is no Word from God that is void of power. We read in Luke 1:37: *"For with God nothing is ever impossible and no word from God shall be without power or impossible of fulfillment"* (AMP). God's Word cannot fail!

Actively Refuse Conditions That Are Contrary to God's Word

It may be that you have a condition in your body that causes you to have continual pain. In the natural, it is difficult to believe God for healing when your body is wracked with pain and disease. However, you must, by faith, actively refuse the conditions that are contrary to God's Word. Doctors may have told you that your sickness is incurable or terminal, but God's Word still declares that by Jesus' stripes, you are healed! (Read Isaiah 53:5.)

If you have a physical infirmity, sickness, or disease, don't talk about it. Sickness is from the devil. When you talk about it, you are acknowledging and glorifying him who put that disease or sickness upon you. Instead of talking about your pain, symptoms, the doctor's report, or complaining about your condition, say what God says. Even when you have contradictory feelings, confess the Word. The Word of God in your mouth is a powerful weapon to defeat satan with. When you declare, "By His stripes I am healed," your words bind satan's hands.

Boldy and firmly rebuke satan. Take authority over the spirits of infirmity and disease. Command them to go, in Jesus' name!

———◄o►———

Claim This Scripture Throughout the Day for Your Healing:

My son, attend to my words; consent and submit to my sayings. Let them not depart from your sight; keep them in the center of your heart. For they are life to those who find them, healing and health to all their flesh (Proverbs 4:20-22 AMP).

———◄o►———

Make the Following Your Confession of Faith:

God's Word is life, healing, and health to my body! Bless the Lord, O my soul. I will not forget all of His benefits. He is Jehovah-rapha, the Lord, my Healer, who forgives all of my iniquities and heals all of my diseases.

Endnotes

1. Smith Wigglesworth, *Smith Wigglesworth on Healing* (New Kensington, PA: Whitaker House, 1999).

2. T.L. Osborn, *Healing the Sick* (Osborn International, 1992).

Day 3

ATTACKING YOUR MIND WITH HIS LIES TO CAUSE YOU TO DOUBT GOD'S LOVE AND HIS WILL TO HEAL YOU

*But without faith it is impossible to please Him:
for he that cometh to God must believe that
He is, and that He is a rewarder of them that
diligently seek Him* (Hebrews 11:6).

Scripture Reading: Matthew 8:2-4

It is the prayer of faith that releases God's healing power. Unless you are convinced that it is God's will to heal, you will be unable to pray the prayer of faith. *"And the prayer of faith shall save the sick, and the Lord shall raise him up"* (James 5:15).

You cannot receive healing for your body until this question is completely settled in your mind.

In Matthew, chapter 8, a leper saw Jesus. He questioned Jesus as to whether it was God's will to heal him or not. He said, "If You are willing, You can make me clean." The leper had most likely heard about Jesus, for news of His power to heal had spread throughout the land. He believed the reports that he had heard concerning Jesus and had no doubts about Christ's ability to heal him of the dreaded leprosy. What he did not know was if Christ would be *willing* to heal him. He said, "If You are willing, You can!"

Moved with compassion Jesus said, "I will!" He healed the man on the spot. There was no hesitation on Jesus' part, no doubt or question as to whether or not it was the will of His Father or if He should heal the leper. He immediately responded to the man's desperate cries, reached out to touch him, and spoke the words, "Be cleansed." As soon as He had spoken, the leprosy immediately left him, and he was cleansed! Sickness and disease had to obey the Word of the Lord!

Satan Will Do Everything Within His Power to Fill Your Mind With His Lies

To receive your healing, you must know (beyond any doubt) that in the same way that Christ was moved with compassion and was willing to heal this leper and all who came to Him over 2,000 years ago, He is willing to heal today. If there is any doubt whatsoever in your mind concerning whether it is God's will to heal you or not, get rid of it now!

Doubt destroys faith. You must believe that the Lord is a Rewarder!

Your mind is satan's major point of attack! It is there that the war must first be fought and won. It is in your mind that satan is unleashing his all-out war. After he attacks your body with sickness and disease, he will bombard your mind with fiery darts of unbelief, fear, worry, confusion, depression, and oppression. He will do everything within his power to fill your mind with his lies concerning God's will to heal you.

Your mind will become so weakened that you will become depressed, frustrated, and filled with a sense of hopelessness and despair.

The moment you begin to worry, you open yourself up for defeat. Satan begins to attack your mind with doubt: If God loves you, why did He allow this sickness? Why is He allowing you to suffer? Why hasn't He healed you? Maybe it isn't God's will to heal you. If God's Word is true, why aren't you healed?

Satan's strategy is to fill your mind so full of fear, worry, and doubt that the Word of God becomes ineffective in your life because it's not mixed with faith. In your circumstances, you have a choice: believe that the sickness satan has brought upon your body will remain;

or refuse to keep your eyes on your circumstances, and believe that God will do exactly what He has promised and heal you.

Knowing That It Is God's Will to Heal You, Take Him at His Word

Your knowledge concerning God's will to heal you cannot be based upon man-made doctrines or traditions. It must be based upon God's Word and His promises concerning healing. Intellectual knowledge is not enough! You must have a revelation. God's Word must come alive within you so that you will be able to come to Him, in full assurance of faith, and believe that He is a Rewarder and will fulfill His promises to heal you.

Knowing His will, because it has been revealed in His Word, when you pray for healing, do not say: "Lord, heal me if it be Your will." This implies doubt. You must come boldly before God. Know that it *is* His will and that He *will* fulfill His promises to heal you. Take Him at His Word. It cannot fail!

Command the Spirits Attacking You to *Go*, in Jesus' Name!

There are thousands of Christians being oppressed in their minds by a spirit of fear. Demonic spirits have afflicted their bodies. They have opened their minds to a spirit of fear concerning their sickness. A spirit of fear is tormenting, oppressing—exercising control over their minds—until they are so bound that they are unable to take hold of God's covenant promise of healing for their bodies.

Don't be passive or timid when dealing with satan and his demonic principalities. Get spiritually aggressive! Through the power of the Holy Spirit, God has given us power *"over all the power of the enemy"* (Luke 10:19). Recognize that the spirits of fear, doubt, worry, depression, intimidation, and fear that are attacking your mind are trespassers that are trying to illegally invade your mind or body to oppress you. Refuse to give them one inch of spiritual territory.

Knowing that through Christ, you have been given power and authority over all of the power of the enemy, command them to *Go*, in Jesus' name!

> *You foul, tormenting spirit of fear, I rebuke you and command you, in the name of Jesus, to loose your hold on my mind. I cast you out by the power and authority that Christ has given to me over you. You will not torment my mind any longer. Your power over me has been broken. You must leave now, in the name of Jesus!*

Spirits of worry, doubt, and unbelief, I command you to loose your hold on my mind. I rebuke you, in the name of Jesus, and command you to leave. You have no power over me. You cannot oppress or trouble my mind any longer. Go! Through the power and authority that Christ has given to me, I cast you out now, in Jesus' name!

You unclean spirits, spirits of infirmity, deaf and dumb spirits, spirits of cancer, diabetes, blindness, and all forms of sickness and disease, I take authority over you now. I command you to loose your hold on my body. In the name of Jesus, I rebuke you and command you to come out! You will not afflict and oppress my body any longer. Christ has paid the price, and with His stripes, I am healed!

Continue to reject every doubt, every thought, every action, and every word that does not line up with God's Word. Knowing that it is God's will to heal you, continue to speak forth God's Word in faith. Confess His promises of healing, and act upon them. As you do, God's healing power will be released and will destroy the disease in your body.

————◄○►————

Claim This Scripture Throughout the Day for Your Healing:

And the prayer of faith shall save the sick, and the Lord shall raise him up (James 5:15).

————◄○►————

Make the Following Your Confession of Faith:

Jesus has redeemed me from the curse. He has destroyed the works of the devil. Sin, sickness, and death have no power over me. Since Christ paid the price by taking the stripes on His back for my healing, I give no place for sickness or pain. I cast out all doubt and fear and receive my healing by faith, in the name of Jesus.

Day 4

CAUSING YOU TO ACCEPT YOUR SICKNESS OR PHYSICAL INFIRMITY

When the even was come, they brought unto Him many that were possessed with devils: and He cast out the spirits with His word, and healed all that were sick (Matthew 8:16).

Scripture Reading: Luke 6:17-29

There is absolutely no foundation for the teaching in the Church today that people who are sick must accept their sickness or disease and resign themselves to being sick, crippled, deaf, blind, or paralyzed.

Jesus never turned one person away or taught anyone that they must resign themselves to being sick. He healed *all* who came to Him. In Luke, we have a beautiful, intimate glimpse of Christ, the Healer, setting people free from all types of diseases: *"And the whole multitude sought to touch Him: for there went virtue out of Him, and healed them all"* (Luke 6:19).

Praise God! Jesus healed them ALL! Wherever Jesus went, as many as touched Him were made whole! *"And whithersoever He entered, into villages, or cities, or country, they laid the sick in the streets, and besought Him that they might touch if it were but the border of His garment: and as many as touched Him were made whole"* (Mark 6:56).

God Sent Jesus to Heal All Who Are Oppressed of the Devil!

Healing of the physical body is equally part of God's plan of redemption. *"How God anointed Jesus of Nazareth with the Holy Ghost and with power: who went about doing good, and healing all that were oppressed of the devil: for God was with Him"* (Acts 10:38). God sent Jesus with this purpose—to heal *all* who were oppressed of the devil!

Jesus laid His healing hand upon all who were brought to Him and healed them all. His power was unlimited! He did not withhold Himself from any of those who came to Him. There was no physical or mental condition, no deformity or paralysis, no sickness or incurable disease that was too difficult or that He could not heal.

You Do Not Have to Carry a Sickness One Day Longer!

Regardless of the sickness, disease, or infirmity that may be afflicting your body, or how long you may have suffered from this affliction, you don't have to continue to carry it.

Satan wants you to give up! He wants you to become weary in persevering in faith for your healing. If you have had a sickness or physical condition for a long time, satan will make you think that since you have prayed and have not received your healing, you must accept it as being God's will or that you must learn to live with it.

Satan is a liar, a thief, and a murderer! Don't listen to him! You don't have to accept sickness and infirmity in your body! Healing is the children's bread! It is part of God's covenant with His people.

There is no physical condition, sickness, or disease that Christ cannot heal! His power to heal is not bound by natural limitations. He can and will heal terminal cancer, malignant brain tumors, kidney failure, liver disease, leukemia, heart disease, multiple sclerosis, bone disease, AIDS, and every other sickness known to man today.

Let Every Struggle Cease!

You may be thinking, *Brother Cerullo, I believe Christ has the power to heal today, but I have prayed, fasted, and have done everything I know to do, yet I am not healed.*

There is a vast difference between *believing* in God's power to heal and having *faith* that He will heal you. The faith that He intends for you to have is not the product of the natural mind. It is not the work of a man. Man cannot manufacture it or work it up. Faith is a supernatural life source that is imparted by God into the life of every believer to manifest the life of Christ.

There is only one Source for faith, and that is Jesus. He is the *"author and finisher of our faith"* (Heb. 12:2). He is the One who imparts it and the One who brings it to full maturity. To receive the supernatural faith of God, you must come to Him. There is no other source and no other way. If you have been struggling to have enough faith to believe God for your healing, let every struggle cease! Get in the presence of the Lord—the Author and Finisher of your faith—until faith is imparted into your heart.

Smith Wigglesworth (who had a dynamic healing ministry in the 1800s) said, "As you are taken up with the glorious fact and the wondrous presence of the living Christ, the faith of God will spring up within you."[1]

Keep Persevering in Faith Until You Receive!

In Luke, chapter 5, we read the story about a paralyzed man who was brought to Peter's house, where Jesus was teaching. There was such a great multitude that they weren't able to find a way to bring him to Jesus; yet, they didn't go away or give up! They persevered through every obstacle—even if it meant going to extreme means and methods to get him to Jesus.

They were fully persuaded that Christ would heal their friend. Faith is a fact, but faith is also an act! They climbed to the roof and drew the man up with ropes on his bed after them. Then they took the tiles off the roof and let the paralyzed man down into the room where Jesus was teaching. Jesus simply spoke the Word, and immediately the man stood to his feet, picked up his bed, and went home, praising God!

As you read this book, let the faith of God arise in your heart! Know that Christ paid the price for your healing and that He is ready to heal you now. Continue to persevere in faith. Instead of accepting the sickness that satan will try to put on you or resigning yourself to live with your infirmity, persevere in faith until you receive your healing. Don't become weary or stop believing and trusting God for your healing. Continue to stand on God's Word! Continue to act in faith!

Continue to rebuke satan, and exercise authority over sickness and disease, in Jesus' name!

———◄o►———

Claim This Scripture Throughout the Day for Your Healing:

For she said within herself, If I may but touch His garment, I shall be whole (Matthew 9:21).

———◄o►———

Make the Following Your Confession of Faith:

Jesus took my infirmities and bore my sicknesses. I refuse to accept my sickness or resign myself to living with any affliction that satan has tried to put on me. I will not give up believing or persevering in faith to touch Christ and be healed.

Endnote

1. Smith Wigglesworth, *Smith Wigglesworth on Healing* (New Kensington, PA: Whitaker House, 1999).

Day 5

BLOCKING YOUR HEALING BY CAUSING YOU TO BE BOUND BY NATURAL LIMITATIONS

Jesus said unto him, If thou canst believe, all things are possible to him that believeth
(Mark 9:23).

Scripture Reading: John 4:46-53

One of the major strategies that satan will try to use to block you from receiving your healing is to try to keep you so focused on natural limitations that you limit what God can do for you. There are many Christians who place limitations on Christ through their limited understanding. They may have been diagnosed with an incurable disease or a terminal illness, inoperable cancer, a physical deformity, paralysis, or may have some long-standing illness that, according to the natural mind, is impossible to recover from. They cannot understand how it could ever be possible for them to be healed.

The nobleman in John, chapter 4, who came to Jesus on behalf of his boy (who was at the point of death), placed limitations on what Christ could do, according to his natural understanding. His faith was stirred when he heard the reports about Jesus healing the sick. He had taken the first step of faith by traveling 20 to 25 miles from Capernaum to Cana, seeking Christ.

When the nobleman found Jesus, he began to beg Jesus to come to his house and heal his son. Like many people today, he had placed limitations upon Christ's power. He believed it was necessary for Christ to personally come to his house and lay His hands upon his son before he could be healed.

Are You Limiting What Christ Will Do for You?

For a moment, think about your circumstances and the healing that you may need in your body. Ask God to reveal if there are any limitations that you have placed upon Christ because of your natural understanding or what you may have been taught concerning healing.

The nobleman's faith was dependent upon an *outward manifestation*—of Christ coming and laying His hands on his son—before he would believe. He did not have his eyes fixed upon Christ's unlimited, immeasurable power but upon an outward manifestation. The nobleman, in his desperation, persisted: *"Sir, come down ere my child die"* (John 4:49).

Jesus did not go with him to his house but required the man to act in faith upon His Word. He said, *"Go thy way; thy son liveth"* (John 4:50). It wasn't necessary for Christ to lay hands on the boy. All that was necessary was for Him to speak the Word! The moment He spoke the Word of healing, the nobleman's son—25 miles away in Capernaum—was healed!

You Must See Christ as He Is Today!

One of the reasons we are not seeing more manifestations of God's healing power in our churches is that we want to see before we believe. Jesus said, *"What things soever ye desire, when ye pray, believe that ye receive them, and ye shall have them"* (Mark 11:24). True faith is believing that you have received *before* you see any outward manifestation!

Friend, Christ wants you to see Him as He is, and believe Him at His Word, even before you see any physical manifestation of your healing. He doesn't want you to see Him just as the One who healed 2,000 years ago or limit His healing power to a time in the past. Neither does He want you to limit Him according to your natural understanding or according to what you see, think, or feel. He wants you to know Him as your Healer!

Think about the people of Nazareth. They limited Christ's power to heal because they saw Him only as a man. Jesus was ready and willing to do a mighty work in their midst, as He had in Capernaum and throughout Galilee (healing the multitudes, opening blind eyes, and healing all manner of disease). They limited Christ because they did not see Him as He is! *"And He could there do no mighty work, save that He laid His hands upon a few sick folk, and healed them"* (Mark 6:5).

There are Christians today who have limited Christ's ability to heal them according to some perception they have in their mind or their lack of knowledge of the Word. They are looking for someone to lay a hand upon them to heal them. They see the miraculous, healing power of God flowing through certain individuals and have their eyes upon the person instead of on Christ, the Healer.

It is time we get our eyes off people...off theology... off doctrines...and get them back on Christ and His unlimited, immeasurable power!

Speak the Word Only!

What a contrast this nobleman's faith is with the Roman centurion's. The centurion came to Jesus on behalf of his servant, who desperately needed healing. The Roman centurion didn't place any limitations on Christ. He saw Jesus as He was—One having supreme power and authority from God over all sicknesses and diseases. He realized that it wasn't necessary for Jesus to come to his house to heal his servant. He believed that all Christ had to do was to speak the Word, and his paralyzed servant, lying in his bed, miles away, would be healed. He told Jesus: *"Speak the word only, and my servant shall be healed"* (Matt. 8:8).

My prayer for you is that God will so anoint your spiritual eyes that you will have a fresh revelation of Christ and see Him as He is today: unlimited, unchanging, all-powerful! When you really see Him and His unlimited power, faith will be released within you to believe Him for the impossible!

In the name of Jesus, break loose from every limitation you have placed upon Christ and His power to heal you. Those things that seem hopeless and impossible with man are possible with God!

The Word for Your Healing Has Already Been Spoken!

The power of God's Word has not changed! *"But He was wounded for our transgressions, He was bruised for our iniquities: the chastisement of our peace was upon Him; and with His stripes we are healed"* (Isa. 53:5). Within this promise is the same creative power that was in the healing Word that Jesus spoke 2,000 years ago!

Just one Word from Him, and blind eyes will open, and He can even create a new eyeball and place it in its socket. One Word from Christ, and dead brain cells are restored, paralyzed limbs are made whole, and diseased kidneys are restored to normal. Praise God! The Word has been spoken! On the cross, Jesus cried, *"It is finished!"* The work for your healing is finished! The price has been paid!

As the Roman centurion saw Christ as He really is (saying, *"Speak the word only, and my servant shall be healed"* in Matthew 8:8), today, you must see Christ in all of the fullness of His mighty power. Begin to speak the Word and His promises of healing into your circumstances and over your body. Remove every natural limitation. Get your eyes on Christ as He is today.

Believe that God will heal you of incurable cancer!

Believe that God will raise you up, out of your wheelchair or bed of affliction!

Whatever need you may have, Christ is saying to you: *"As thou hast believed, so be it done unto thee"* (Matt. 8:13). There are no limitations upon God's power. It is according to what you can believe for, and act in faith to receive.

————◄○►————

Claim This Scripture Throughout the Day for Your Healing:

And ye shall serve the Lord your God, and He shall bless thy bread, and thy water; and I will take sickness away from the midst of thee (Exodus 23:25).

————◄○►————

Make the Following Your Confession of Faith:

Because I have made the Lord, who is my refuge, my habitation, there shall no evil befall me. Neither shall any plague, sickness, or disease come near my dwelling. I will walk in the provision of His healing for my life.

Day 6

CAUSING YOUR FAITH TO WAVER

But let him ask in faith, nothing wavering. For he that wavereth is like a wave of the sea driven with the wind and tossed. For let not that man think that he shall receive any thing from the Lord (James 1:6-7).

Scripture Reading: Matthew 17:14-21 and Mark 9:14-29

To receive your healing, your faith must be so rooted in God's promises concerning His divine healing that absolutely nothing will be able to shake you. You must not waver according to what you think, what you hear, what you feel, or what the symptoms of the disease in your body are. The moment you begin to waver, unbelief establishes a stronghold. This will hinder you from acting in faith on God's Word.

There are many Christians who do not receive their healing because their faith wavers. They pray and stand on God's promises concerning healing, but when they do not see immediate results or changes in their physical condition, they begin to doubt and question God's Word. They may believe the Word, and accept their healing, as long as they can see a manifestation of their healing, but as soon as symptoms appear, or they feel pain, their faith wavers. They cast out the Word, stop believing and confessing the promises of God, and start confessing their sickness and talking about their symptoms, which annuls the prayer of faith.

The key to receiving from God is the absence of doubt! *"But without faith it is impossible to please Him: for he that cometh to God must believe that He is, and that He is a rewarder of them that diligently seek Him"* (Heb. 11:6). Satan's goal is to cause your faith in God and His healing power to waver so that you will fail to act in faith on His Word. James said that if we waver, we will not be able to receive anything from the Lord! (See James 1:6-7.)

There may be times when the pain you feel in your body is so intense, or your circumstances are so difficult, that you are no longer exercising faith for your healing. As the intensity of your suffering increases, it causes you to focus on yourself and the pain. You begin to rely on natural methods, doctors, and medicines for relief, instead of focusing on Christ and His provision for your healing.

Lord, Help My Unbelief!

The man who brought his demon-possessed boy to be healed was so focused on the physical condition of his son that his faith was wavering. When he brought his son to the disciples, they were unable to cast the demon out. The scribes were arguing with the disciples, trying to disprove and deny the power of Christ.

That's when Christ came on the scene.

It was clear why the boy had not been healed. Jesus looked at the multitude and rebuked their unbelief: *"O faithless generation, how long shall I be with you? how long shall I suffer you? bring him unto Me"* (Mark 9:19).

They brought the boy to Jesus. The father was desperate. His son was in such torment that he was wasting away before his father's eyes. There was nothing the father could do, in the natural. The disciples had been unable to cast the demon out. He was there at the feet of Jesus, crying out for His mercy and compassion to heal his son; yet, the man's faith was wavering. He said, *"If Thou canst do any thing, have compassion on us, and help us"* (Mark 9:22). He made his son's healing dependent upon Jesus' power to heal. His healing was not dependent upon Jesus' power or His willingness to heal. It was dependent upon one thing—the father's ability to believe!

Jesus placed the responsibility back upon the father. He said, *"If thou canst believe, all things are possible to him that believeth"* (Mark 9:23). The man cried out, *"Lord, I believe; help Thou mine unbelief"* (Mark 9:24). He knew he needed Christ to help him to overcome the unbelief that was still in his heart. Full of compassion, Jesus responded to his cry, rebuked the devil in his son, and cast it out. *"And the child was cured from that very hour"* (Matt. 17:18).

No More Doubt!

It is not enough to pray and ask God for your healing. Praying without faith is powerless. It is the prayer of faith that saves the sick. (See James 5:15.) When you come before God, you must believe that He is a Rewarder, that He will reward your faith and release His healing power into your body. When you waver, your faith is up one day and down the next, depending upon how you feel, according to your circumstances, or according to the symptoms of the disease or physical condition of your body.

If you are going to receive healing, you must have faith and doubt not! When you ask in faith, according to His will, you can have full confidence, be fully persuaded, and *know* that you will receive whatever you ask!

> *And this is the confidence that we have in Him, that, if we ask any thing according to His will, He heareth us: And if we know that He hear us, whatsoever we ask, we know that we have the petitions that we desired of Him* (1 John 5:14-15).

If You Can Believe, All Things Are Possible!

Knowing that Christ took your infirmities and bore your sicknesses in His own body (see Matt. 8:17), by His stripes, you *are* healed! (See First Peter 2:24.) Come to Him in faith. Fully surrender yourself, including your sickness and your physical condition, completely and totally into His hands. Trust and believe that He will heal you.

Your healing has already been provided for and is not dependent upon Christ's power or His willingness to heal you. It is dependent upon whether or not you will act in faith, upon His promises, and believe Him. Whatever healing you may need in your body, Christ is ready and willing to heal you now. He is saying to you, "If you can believe, all things are possible!" If you can believe, you can be healed today—right now—as you are reading this book. You don't have to wait one minute longer!

If there is a struggle in your heart to have faith that Christ will heal you, cry out to Him, "Lord, I believe! Help my unbelief!" Get rid of every trace of unbelief. Take God at His Word and act in faith on His promises. Without waiting to feel better or to see a physical manifestation of your healing, claim it in faith, and begin to praise God for it.

———◄○►———

Claim This Scripture Throughout the Day for Your Healing. Say With David:

O Lord my God, I cried unto Thee, and Thou hast healed me (Psalm 30:2).

———◄○►———

Make the Following Your Confession of Faith:

I will not be moved by my circumstances, pain, or symptoms. I cast out every trace of doubt, in Jesus' name, and receive my healing now. Since Christ paid the price for my healing, I will reject every negative thought and every lie of satan. By faith, I declare that I am healed!

FAILURE TO ACT IN FAITH AND OBEDIENCE ON GOD'S PROMISES

If ye have faith as a grain of mustard seed, ye shall say unto this mountain, Remove hence to yonder place; and it shall remove; and nothing shall be impossible unto you (Matthew 17:20).

Scripture Reading: Second Kings 5:1-14

What are the things in your life that seem impossible?

Are you suffering from an incurable sickness or disease?

Do you have a physical condition that can only be met by a supernatural manifestation of God's power?

Christ has already made full provision for your healing! It is His will to heal you! He stands ready and willing to heal all who come to Him in faith. However, your healing is dependent upon whether or not you will act in faith upon His promises.

Faith is a fact, but faith is also an act! It is not enough to say that you **believe** God's promises. Faith that does not result in action is not faith at all! James wrote: *"Even so faith, if it hath not works, is dead, being alone"* (James 2:17). Smith Wigglesworth (referred to as "the apostle of faith") said: "Faith is actively refusing the power of the devil. It is not saying mere words. You must have an activity of faith, refusing the conditions, in the name of Jesus."[1]

One of satan's major strategies to block your healing is to hinder you from putting your faith into action. There are many people who hear about Jesus and His power to heal but fail to act in faith upon the Word and never receive their healing.

Naaman's Act of Faith and Obedience Brought Healing

One of the clearest examples of the importance of acting in faith and obedience to the Word of the Lord to receive healing is the healing of Naaman. In Second Kings, chapter 5, we read that Naaman, captain of the host of Syria, had leprosy. An Israelite girl, serving as a maid in Naaman's household, told Naaman's wife about a prophet who would heal him of his leprosy. The king of Syria sent him to the king of Israel to ask him to cure

Naaman's leprosy. Elisha sent a message to the king saying: *"Have the man come to me and he will know that there is a prophet in Israel"* (2 Kings 5:8 NIV).

When Naaman arrived at Elisha's house to have him pray for his healing, Elisha didn't even come out to meet him. He sent a messenger to Naaman to tell him to go and wash seven times in the Jordan River. When Naaman heard the message, he was filled with anger and went away in a rage. It wasn't until he received the Word of the Lord, spoken by Elisha, and acted in obedience to what he was directed to do that he was healed.

Going through a form or ritual of bathing in the Jordan seven times isn't what enabled Naaman to receive his healing. It was his willingness to act, in faith and obedience, on the Word of the Lord that had been spoken through Elisha.

Your Healing Is Dependent Upon Putting Your Faith Into Action

In every example of healing that God has given to us in His Word, regardless of the method used, it was the act or expression of faith that enabled the individual to receive the miracle of healing that he needed.

- Jesus commanded the man sick with the palsy: *"Arise, take up thy bed, and go unto thine house"* (Matt. 9:6).

- He told the impotent man at the pool of Bethesda: *"Rise, take up thy bed, and walk"* (John 5:8).

- He said to the man with the withered hand: *"Stretch forth thine hand"* (Matt. 12:13).

- He said to the blind man: *"Go, wash in the pool of Siloam"* (John 9:7).

To receive their healing, it was necessary for those who came to Jesus to act upon the Word that He spoke to them.

Knowing that God's creative power is in His Word, you must simply believe it, and act on it! This is one of the most important keys to receiving healing. Knowing that it is God's will to heal you, you must believe, and act in faith! Refuse to allow satan to hinder you from putting your faith into action.

Turn Away From All Dependence Upon Your Natural Resources

Satan will hinder you from putting your faith into action by trying to make you continue to rely on your natural mind and natural resources. What God directed Naaman to do through Elisha was in direct contrast to this man's logic and understanding. It didn't make any sense to him. He said, *"I thought that he would surely come out to me and stand and call on the name of the Lord his God, wave his hand over the spot and cure me of my leprosy"* (2 Kings 5:11 NIV).

The natural mind cannot comprehend the things of God. *"But the natural man receiveth not the things of the Spirit of God: for they are foolishness unto him: neither can he know them, because they are spiritually discerned"* (1 Cor. 2:14). To the natural mind, it was impossible that by simply dipping in the river Jordan, Naaman would be healed of leprosy. There were no healing powers in the water. If there were, then all of the lepers throughout the land would have been able to come and be cleansed.

Totally Surrender to God, and Act in Faith on His Promises for Your Healing

You must come to the place where you are no longer dependent upon your natural resources. You must totally surrender your life into God's hands and trust in His supernatural power to heal you. There are Christians today who are looking to every possible natural resource, trying to find relief and a cure for the afflictions in their body. They are depending upon modern medical technology, doctors, medicines, and remedies for their healing instead of acting in faith on God's promises of healing.

We believe in medical science and thank God for good doctors. We thank God for medical science and its advanced technology that is helping to overcome diseases and sicknesses. However, we also believe that there is only one Power in Heaven and earth that has the final Word regarding the healing of our diseases and afflictions. It is God. Only God can heal!

It wasn't until Naaman turned away from his dependence upon his natural understanding, submitted himself totally to God, and acted in faith that he was healed. The seventh time he dipped himself (according to the Word of the Lord that was spoken by Elisha), Naaman came out of the water, the dreaded leprosy was gone, and he had new skin, like that of a baby.

It is only when you come to the end of yourself, turn away from your dependence upon the natural, and lean completely on God for His divine healing power to heal you that will you be able to take the step of faith necessary to reach out and touch Christ to receive the healing that you need.

Activate Your Faith Through Your Obedience!

There is a vast difference between the type of faith that the majority of professing Christians have today and the faith that Jesus taught that was able to move mountains. In that realm of faith, nothing is impossible!

One type of faith ends in talk. True faith is manifested in deeds.

One crumbles under trials and afflictions. True faith withstands all opposition and every trial.

One is inoperative and produces no results. True faith is active and powerful!

Put your faith into action by acting on God's promise of healing to you.

God's Word declares that by the stripes (which Christ took upon His back), you are healed! You must look to Christ, and act in faith and obedience to whatever He directs you to do. If He directs you to take your hearing aid off, expect Him to heal you. Put your faith into action, and do it, even before there is a manifestation of your healing. If you are confined to a wheelchair, unable to walk unaided, as the healing power of God flows into your body, put your faith into action. Make every effort to rise up out of that wheelchair and begin to walk, in Jesus' name!

The power for the fulfillment of every promise of God is in His Word. As you act in faith upon God's Word, His healing power will be released. It will set you free from sicknesses and diseases!

The Word for Your Healing Has Already Been Spoken!

The work has been done! Everything necessary for the manifestation of the healing that you need in your body, or in the life of your loved ones, has already been accomplished! It's up to you now to respond. Put your faith into action upon the Word that God has already spoken.

You have a choice. You can look upon Christ (who bore your sins and sicknesses upon Himself, and by whose stripes you are healed), believe and act upon the Word, and be healed; or, you can keep your eyes on your symptoms, listen to the lies of the enemy, and remain sick.

Activate your faith through your acts of obedience. Don't hesitate or follow your own will instead of obeying God. All acts of self-will are rebellion against God. They will block the flow and hinder you from taking possession of your healing. Whatever God asks you to do, don't question it or try to determine why, just obey. Faith and obedience to the Word of the Lord activate the release of God's healing power.

In Acts chapter 9, we read that Peter said to Aeneas (who had been a paralytic for eight years): *"Jesus Christ maketh thee whole: arise, and make thy bed"* (Acts 9:34). Aeneas did not look at his hopeless condition. He did not say to Peter, I've been paralyzed for eight years, and there is no way that I can get up from here and walk. The Word says that Aeneas immediately obeyed and rose from his bed. He was healed! He obeyed, put his faith into action, and his healing was complete.

Receive the Word of God, and believe that God will do exactly what He has promised to do. As you receive the Word, speak it forth in faith. Act in obedience if

God is asking you to do something that you haven't been able to do. Believe that you have received your healing, even before you see a visible manifestation. Continue to persevere in faith until your healing is complete.

————◄o►————

Claim This Scripture Throughout the Day for Your Healing:

> *How God anointed Jesus of Nazareth with the Holy Ghost and with power: who went about doing good, and healing all that were oppressed of the devil* (Acts 10:38).

————◄o►————

Make the Following Your Confession of Faith:

> *Father, Your Word says that You anointed Jesus and sent Him to heal all who were oppressed by the devil. I believe that Jesus came to save and to heal me and that my healing is provided for in the Atonement. I receive my healing now by faith and act on Your Word to take possession of all that You have provided for me.*

Endnote

1. Smith Wigglesworth, *Smith Wigglesworth on Healing* (New Kensington, PA: Whitaker House, 1999).

Part II

GOD'S SEVENFOLD CONTRACT OF DIVINE HEALING!

Day 8

HEALING PROVISION #1

He sent His word, and healed them, and
delivered them from their destructions
(Psalm 107:20).

Scripture Reading: Exodus 15:23-25 and 23:25

God has entered an everlasting covenant—which provides for all of your needs, ***including your healing***—and has bound Himself to you with His Word. He promised: *"I will make a covenant of peace with them; it shall be an everlasting covenant with them"* (Ezek. 37:26) and *"My covenant will I not break, nor alter the thing that is gone out of My lips"* (Ps. 89:34).

From His very first dealings with the children of Israel, God's purpose was to remove sickness from among His people. He entered a covenant of healing with them in the wilderness.

God told His people:

> *If thou wilt diligently hearken to the voice of the Lord thy God, and wilt do that which is right in His sight, and wilt give ear to His commandments, and keep all His statutes, I will put none of these diseases upon thee, which I have brought upon the Egyptians: for I am the Lord that healeth thee* (Exodus 15:26).

God wanted His people to know that not only was He their mighty Deliverer, but He was *Jehovah-rapha,* the God who would heal them. In this covenant, He made them a promise. He told them that He would not put on them any of the diseases that He had put upon the Egyptians in delivering them out of bondage.

God Promised to Remove Sickness From His People

Later, on Mount Sinai, after God had spoken and given them the Ten Commandments, He promised: *"I will take sickness away from the midst of thee"* (Exod. 23:25). Forty years later, as they prepared to enter the land that God had promised would be theirs, Moses reminded them of this covenant and God's promise of healing.

Moses said:

> *Wherefore it shall come to pass, if ye hearken to these judgments, and keep, and do them, that the Lord thy God shall keep unto thee the covenant and the mercy which He sware unto thy fathers....Thou shalt be blessed above all people: there shall not be male or female barren among you, or among your cattle. And the Lord will take away from thee all sickness, and will put none of the evil diseases of Egypt, which thou knowest, upon thee; but will lay them upon all them that hate thee* (Deuteronomy 7:12,14-15).

Our God Is a Healing God!

God has planned for His people to be free from sickness and disease and to live in divine health! When the children of Israel entered the Promised Land, there was not one feeble person among them. *"He brought them forth also with silver and gold: and there was not one feeble person among their tribes"* (Ps. 105:37).

In the same way that God entered a covenant with Israel that included their healing and the removal of sickness from among them, He has entered a covenant with you that provides for your healing. He has made a contract with you that guarantees your healing!

There are many promises in God's Word for you to claim for your healing, but for the next seven days, I want you to focus on seven provisions which are part of God's contract for your healing. Read each of these seven provisions daily. Act in faith on them. Believe and expect God to heal you and your loved ones.

God Sent His Word—the Written and the Living Word—to Heal!

God sent forth Jesus, the living Word, to reverse the curse that had come upon humankind because of his sinful disobedience. God never intended for man to experience sin, sickness, or death. These are a result of the curse.

God sent forth the Word:

> *In the beginning was the Word, and the Word was with God, and the Word was God....And the Word was made flesh, and dwelt among us, (and we beheld His glory, the glory as of the only begotten of the Father,) full of grace and truth* (John 1:1,14).

He sent forth the Word—Jesus Christ—to destroy the works of the devil and redeem humankind from the bondage of sin, sickness, and death. *"For this purpose the Son of God was manifested, that He might destroy the works of the devil"* (1 John 3:8).

The Living Word Broke the Power of Sin, Sickness, and Death!

Through His death on the cross, Jesus became the only acceptable sacrifice sufficient to break the bondage of sin, sickness, and death from humankind and restore us back to God. He freely gave Himself that we might be set free from all of the power of satan!

Jesus arose triumphantly. He had retrieved the keys of death, hell, and the grave. He fulfilled the purpose for which He had been sent. He destroyed the works of the devil, and He is now seated at the right hand of the Father in a position of power and glory over every principality and power!

God sent His Word—the living Word—and broke the power of sin, sickness, and death from humankind. *"And He went about all Galilee, teaching in their synagogues and preaching the good news (Gospel) of the kingdom, and healing every disease and every weakness and infirmity among the people"* (Matt. 4:23 AMP).

God Desires to Release a Continual Flow of His Healing Power Into Your Life!

Friend, this is the solid foundation upon which you are able to stand in faith, and claim your healing. God has made a contract with you and forever sealed it with the blood of Jesus. However, before you can benefit from the provisions in this contract, you must take it by faith, and begin to apply the promises that are contained within it.

Not only does God want you to be healed from the afflictions and diseases that the devil will try to put on you, He wants you to be covered with His healing power, from the top of your head to the soles of your feet!

It is His will that there be a continual release and flow of His divine, healing power into your life to keep sickness away!

God is ready to heal you now and release a divine flow of His healing power into your body. However, you must take God's contract for your healing, and act on it. Your act of faith activates and releases His healing power into your life.

————◄◦►————

Claim Psalm 107:20. It Is a Part of God's Contract for Your Healing.

He sent His word, and healed them, and delivered them from their destructions (Psalm 107:20).

Read it aloud throughout the day. Meditate on it, and claim this promise by faith.

————◄o►————

Make the Following Your Confession of Faith:

The God that I serve is Jehovah-rapha, the God who heals me of all of my sicknesses and diseases. Today, I take hold of God's contract for my healing with all of its provisions. God sent His Word and has healed me!

Day 9

HEALING PROVISION #2

Surely He hath borne our griefs, and carried our sorrows: yet we did esteem Him stricken, smitten of God, and afflicted. But He was wounded for our transgressions, He was bruised for our iniquities: the chastisement of our peace was upon Him; and with His stripes we are healed (Isaiah 53:4-5).

Scripture Reading: Isaiah 53:1-12 and Deuteronomy 7:9-15

Before you can act in faith to break satan's sevenfold attack against your body, you must know what is in the contract that God has given to you, which provides for your healing. A contract is a legally binding agreement between two or more parties. The individual who draws up the contract lists the services or goods that they will provide, as well as the terms or conditions of the agreement, which must be followed. The contract does not become final until both parties have signed it.

God's Word is His contract with you, in which He has revealed His provisions for your healing. In both the Old and New Testaments, God's Word clearly reveals that His plan of restoration for humankind not only provides salvation from sins but also for healing.

Everything that is required for you to be healed has been accomplished by Christ's sacrifice of Himself upon the cross. It's recorded in the contract! He did not lay down His life, carry your sins and sicknesses, and suffer the shame and agony of the cross for you to experience a 50 percent, a 75 percent, or even a 95 percent victory over the devil. He made it possible for you, through His contract, to experience healing and restoration in every area of your life.

Christ Bore Your Sicknesses and Carried Your Pains

More than 700 years before Jesus was born, Isaiah prophesied concerning Christ, His coming, His sufferings on the cross, and the promised healing and deliverance that would come through that sacrifice.

Isaiah, chapter 53, contains part of God's contract for your healing. Jesus fulfilled the prophecy!

Let's look closely at Isaiah 53:4: *"Surely He hath borne our griefs, and carried our sorrows...."* The word "griefs" in the original Hebrew text is the word *choli,* which is more accurately translated "sicknesses." The word "sorrows" is translated from the Hebrew word *makob,* meaning "pains." These two words, *choli* and *makob,* everywhere else in the Old Testament mean "sicknesses" and "pains." Therefore, Isaiah was saying in verse 4, *"Surely He hath borne our* **[sicknesses]** *and carried our* **[pains]**.*"* Neither of these words translated "sicknesses" and "pains" have any reference to spiritual matters but specifically and only bodily sickness.

Christ Lifted—Removed—*Your* Sin, Sicknesses, and Pains!

Now look at the word "borne" in Isaiah 53:4. It is translated from the Hebrew word *nasa* meaning "to lift up," "to bear away," "to convey," or "to remove to a distance." When Jesus bore your sin, sicknesses, and pains, He lifted them. This isn't referring to Jesus symbolically carrying or lifting our sin, sicknesses, and pain. It refers to an actual substitution for and a complete removal of them!

Christ Paid the Price and Took *Your* Place!

Friend, this is a provision of God's contract of healing for you!

Regardless of the infirmity, sickness, or disease that may be afflicting your body, Jesus took *your* place.

He paid the penalty for *your* sins **and** sicknesses by lifting them off you and taking them upon Himself.

Since He has lifted them off you, you don't have to carry them any longer!

F.F. Bosworth (who wrote the powerful classic, *Christ, the Healer)* said, "It is not meant that the Servant of Jehovah merely entered into a fellowship of our sufferings, but that He took on Himself the sufferings that we had to bear and deserved to bear."[1]

Are you ready to be healed?

Now Is the Time! Today Is Your Day!

Release your faith! Claim God's contract of healing, and act on it now!

Focus your vision on Christ, your Healer. See Him carrying your sicknesses and pains upon Himself.

Believe that His supreme sacrifice was sufficient to redeem you from all sin and to heal your body.

God is a Spirit. He is everywhere present. He is right by your side and is ready and willing to heal you now!

Receive your healing by faith, and begin to praise Him for it now.

————◄o►————

Claim Isaiah 53:4-5. It Contains Part of God's Contract for Your Healing.

Surely He hath borne our griefs, and carried our sorrows: yet we did esteem Him stricken, smitten of God, and afflicted. But He was wounded for our transgressions, He was bruised for our iniquities: the chastisement of our peace was upon Him; and with His stripes we are healed (Isaiah 53:4-5).

Meditate on these verses throughout the day, and act in faith upon them.

————◄o►————

Make the Following Your Confession of Faith:

Jesus took my place. He lifted and removed my sin, sickness, and pains. He was wounded for my transgressions and was bruised for my iniquities. The chastisement of my peace was upon Him, and with His stripes, I am healed!

Endnote

1. F.F. Bosworth, *Christ, The Healer* (Grand Rapids, MI: Revell Co., 1983).

Day 10

HEALING PROVISION #3

When the even was come, they brought unto Him many that were possessed with devils: and He cast out the spirits with His word, and healed all that were sick: That it might be fulfilled which was spoken by Esaias the prophet, saying, Himself took our infirmities, and bare our sicknesses (Matthew 8:16-17).

Scripture Reading: Matthew 4:23-24

God's contract for divine healing was revealed, demonstrated, and made effective through Christ. As God revealed Himself to the children of Israel through His redemptive name, *Jehovah-tsidkenu,* Christ came in His Father's name and revealed Himself to be *Jehovah-rapha,* "the God who healeth thee."

Jesus said, *"I am come in My Father's name"* (John 5:43). He manifested the fullness of His Father's name! As he reached out to suffering humanity, healed the sick, opened blind eyes, unstopped deaf ears, caused the lame to walk, and raised the dead, He manifested His Father's name and revealed the Father's plan concerning divine healing.

Everywhere Jesus went, God's divine, healing power flowed through Him to heal the sick. From the very beginning of His ministry, until the day that He went to the cross, He was lifting sicknesses and diseases from all who came to Him.

Jesus Took *Your* Infirmities and Bore *Your* Sicknesses

In Matthew 8:16-17 we read that Jesus' healing the sick was a fulfillment of Isaiah's prophecy that Christ would take the sicknesses and infirmities of man upon Himself. Notice that Matthew interpreted what Isaiah wrote in Isaiah 53:4, *"Surely He hath borne our griefs, and carried our sorrows,"* as it is translated in the original Hebrew, *"Himself took our infirmities, and bare our sicknesses"* (Matt. 8:17). Matthew gave a firsthand testimony that Jesus healed all who were sick *"that it might be fulfilled which was spoken by Esaias the prophet..."* (Matt. 8:17).

Jesus took every form of sickness and disease known to man upon Himself. This not only included the diseases that were mentioned in the curse of the law (see Deut. 28:15-62), but also: cancer, leukemia, diabetes, AIDS, heart and lung disease, liver disease, arthritis, multiple sclerosis, blindness, deafness, crippling diseases, schizophrenia, manic depression, shingles, and every other disease and sickness in the world today.

Whatever infirmity, sickness, disease, or affliction you may have, it is illegal! Jesus took them upon Himself!

There Is Healing in Christ's Presence!

Through the power of the Holy Spirit within Christ, there was a flow of the divine life of God that was released through Him to forgive man's sins, heal the sick, open blind eyes, cleanse the leper, and raise the dead! When Jesus began His ministry, He preached about the Kingdom of God and healed the sick! There was no sickness or condition that was too difficult for Him to heal. He healed all manner of sickness and disease—without exception!

The anointing of the Holy Spirit—the *dunamis* power of God—was so strong that people were healed simply by Him speaking a Word, laying hands on them, or by them simply touching the hem of His garment.

There was healing power in His presence! As the people heard about Jesus and His power to heal, multitudes came to hear Him teach and to be healed.

But so much the more went there a fame abroad of Him: and great multitudes came together to hear, and to be healed by Him of their infirmities....And it came to pass on a certain day, as He was teaching, that there were Pharisees and doctors of the law sitting by, which were come out of every town of Galilee, and Judaea, and Jerusalem: and the power of the Lord was present to heal them (Luke 5:15,17).

Jesus Fulfilled Isaiah's Prophecy!

When He began His ministry, Jesus went into the synagogue in Nazareth, picked up the scroll containing Isaiah's prophecy concerning the Messiah, and began to read:

The Spirit of the Lord is upon Me, because He hath anointed Me to preach the gospel to the poor; He hath sent Me to heal the brokenhearted, to preach deliverance to the captives, and recovering of sight to the blind, to set at liberty them that are bruised, to preach the acceptable year of the Lord (Luke 4:18-19).

With all eyes fastened upon Him, He closed the book, and said, *"This day is this scripture fulfilled in your ears"* (Luke 4:21).

Jesus knew that God had anointed Him *"with the Holy Ghost and with power"* (Acts 10:38). He understood that He had been sent to *"destroy the works of the devil"* (1 John 3:8). Jesus took authority over the sicknesses and diseases that were upon the people who came to Him for healing. He rebuked them and spoke the Word of healing and deliverance. As the anointing of the Holy Spirit flowed through Him, God's power was released, and the bondages of sickness and disease were broken!

Get Into His Presence!

Today, wherever the Spirit of God is flowing, His presence is present to heal!

You can be healed and set free from the sickness and disease you may be carrying in your body, once and for all! Shut everything else out of your heart and mind. See Jesus lifting your sickness from you. Get into His presence, and begin to pray. As the same resurrected, life-giving Spirit that was released through Christ is flowing, release your faith. Let His divine, healing power pour life into your body.

In the name of Jesus, take authority over the sickness and disease in your body or mind, or in the body or mind of your loved one. Rebuke the spirits of infirmity and disease or mental confusion, fear, anxiety, and torment. Command them to loose their hold on you now in the name of Jesus!

———◄○►———

Claim the Provision of Matthew 8:16-17. It Is Part of God's Contract for Your Healing:

> *When the even was come, they brought unto Him many that were possessed with devils: and He cast out the spirits with His word, and healed all that were sick: That it might be fulfilled which was spoken by Esaias the prophet, saying, Himself took our infirmities, and bare our sicknesses* (Matthew 8:16-17).

———◄○►———

Make the Following a Confession of Your Faith and What You Believe God Will Do for You:

> *God sent Jesus to break the bondage of sin, sickness, and disease. He took my infirmities and bore my sicknesses. The sickness and disease in my body*

is illegal! Therefore, I refuse to allow it to have dominion. By faith, I receive the life-giving flow of God's healing power into my body now, setting me free from all pain, sickness, suffering, and disease, in Jesus' name!

Day 11

HEALING PROVISION #4

Who His own self bare our sins in His own body on the tree, that we, being dead to sins, should live unto righteousness: by whose stripes ye were healed (1 Peter 2:24).

Scripture Reading: Numbers 21:4-9 and First Peter 2:21-24

Christ has lifted your sins and sicknesses from you. By the wounds He bore on His own body, you were healed! Past tense! It's already done!

As soldiers stripped Jesus' robe from Him and beat His back with 39 stripes with cat-o'-nine tails, He took those stripes for your healing. See Him there, blood coursing down His back, and the Roman soldiers mercilessly beating Him until His muscles were shredded. *"His appearance was so disfigured beyond that of any man and His form marred beyond human likeness"* (Isa. 52:14 NIV).

As they pierced His side, nailed His hands (wrists) and feet to the cross, lifted it, and shoved it into the ground, the blood poured forth. With every drop of blood that was being shed, He was setting you free. He became a curse for you.

> *Christ hath redeemed us from the curse of the law, being made a curse for us: for it is written, Cursed is every one that hangeth on a tree: That the blessing of Abraham might come on the Gentiles through Jesus Christ; that we might receive the promise of the Spirit through faith* (Galatians 3:13-14).

The Curse Has Been Broken!

Christ was lifted up on the cross and became a curse for humankind. He bore your sins and sicknesses in His own body. He paid the supreme price to redeem you from your sins and provide healing for your body. God's contract for your healing has been signed with the blood of Jesus, making it effective and irrevocable!

Jesus said concerning His death: *"And as Moses lifted up the serpent in the wilderness, even so must the Son of man be lifted up: That whosoever believeth in Him should not perish, but have eternal life"* (John 3:14-15). He also said, *"And I, if I be lifted up from the earth, will draw all men unto Me. This He said, signifying what death He should die"* (John 12:32-33).

God Provided Healing for Everyone!

God made a covenant of healing with the children of Israel whereby they would be able to walk in divine healing. God would remove sickness from them, if they would obey Him and keep His commandments and statutes.

However, the people soon forgot His covenant. Instead of looking to Him, their Source, and believing and trusting that He would fulfill His promises, they began to accuse God and to murmur and complain. As a result of their rebellion God sent fiery serpents among them, and many of them died. They brought God's judgment upon themselves through their rebellion.

In His great love and mercy, when the people turned to Him in repentance, God provided a way of healing for them. God directed Moses to make a brazen serpent and to place it upon a pole. All who looked upon it would be healed from the curse of the plague. The children of Israel were living under a curse for their rebellion and disobedience. By looking at the brass serpent on the pole, the curse was removed, and the people were healed.

God told Moses that everyone who looked upon it would live. He provided healing for everyone. They had a choice. They could look upon the brass serpent on the pole, and live; or refuse to look upon it, and die. God made it perfectly clear that only those who looked upon the brazen serpent would live.

There, in the wilderness, over a thousand years before Christ was born, God wanted His people to learn to look to Him and trust Him for their healing. This brazen serpent on a pole was a type of the healing and deliverance that God planned to send as the result of Christ becoming a curse, being crucified, and being lifted up on the cross to remove the curse of sin that was upon humankind.

Christ's Blood Sealed God's Covenant of Healing

Praise God! Christ has broken the curse! As He was lifted up on the cross (becoming a curse for human-kind, bearing your sins and sicknesses in His own body), He paid the supreme price to redeem you from your sins and to provide healing for your body.

The blood that poured forth that day from Jesus' body completely abolished the curse of the law and put into effect the new covenant—with all of its provisions for forgiveness, deliverance, freedom, healing, and all of the other covenant promises. The covenant promises are not dependent upon whether or not you have enough faith to believe them. They are true and just as powerful today as the day God spoke them into existence. They are dependent upon the power of the blood that Jesus shed for us.

All of God's promises (including First Peter 2:24, which says, *"Who His own self bare our sins in His own body on the tree, that we, being dead to sins, should live unto righteousness: by whose stripes ye were healed"*) are your inheritance! They have been sealed, secured, and made legally binding with Christ's blood and with an oath that God has made. He has promised: *"My covenant will I not break, nor alter the thing that is gone out of My lips"* (Ps. 89:34).

You Have a Choice!

Today, you have been set free from the curse of the law. Through Christ, you have the forgiveness of your sins and healing for your body!

Everyone who looked upon the brazen serpent on the pole in the wilderness was healed. Today, everyone who looks upon Jesus as their Healer and believes in Him will have their sins forgiven and can reach out in faith for their healing.

You have a choice—receive God's provision of healing by faith, and look to Jesus, expecting to be healed; or, through your unbelief, accept your sickness, and remain in your present condition.

You must take hold of God's contract (signed with God's oath and sealed with the blood of Jesus) by faith. Get your eyes off your physical condition—the pain and symptoms of your disease and what your natural mind believes—and look upon Jesus on the cross, paying the price so that you can be healed today.

It Is Finished!

On the cross, Jesus cried, *"It is finished."* The work was done. Your healing was complete. With His stripes, you were healed! There is absolutely nothing left that needs to be done for your salvation and healing.

Let every struggle of your heart cease. Get into His presence. Focus your heart and mind on Him and Him alone for your healing. Act in faith on what God has revealed in His contract of healing. Shut out the negative voices of doubt and unbelief.

Reach out to Him right now, and be healed, in His mighty name!

———————◄o►———————

Release Your Faith, and Claim the Provision of First Peter 2:24. It Is Part of God's Contract for Your Healing.

Who His own self bare our sins in His own body on the tree, that we, being dead to sins, should live unto righteousness: by whose stripes ye were healed (1 Peter 2:24).

———————◄o►———————

Make the Following Confession of Your Faith Throughout the Day. Believe That God's Healing Power Will Be Released Into Your Body:

God's contract for my healing has been signed with the blood of Jesus. Christ has broken the curse of sin, sickness, and disease off my life. He paid the supreme price to redeem me from sin and heal my body. My healing was paid for on the cross, and nothing remains undone. By His stripes, I **have been** *healed!*

Day 12

HEALING PROVISION #5

Bless the Lord; O my soul, and forget not all His benefits: who forgiveth all thine iniquities; who healeth all thy diseases (Psalm 103:2-3).

Scripture Reading: Mark 2:1-12

The all-powerful God who entered into a covenant with Israel and promised to take sickness and disease from their midst is the same God who has placed His Spirit within you! It is His will to release a flow of His divine, healing power within your life so that there will be a continual stream flowing through you for salvation, healing, deliverance, and for meeting your every need. Total healing!

The same life-giving flow of the Spirit that was released through Jesus to open blind eyes, heal all manner of sicknesses and diseases, that caused the lame to walk and raised the dead, is flowing in you—not only to forgive your sins and manifest Christ's life within your spirit, but to heal your physical body.

God Sent Jesus to Save *and to Heal!*

Healing the physical body is equally part of God's plan of redemption. The same power of God that forgives us of our sins also heals our bodies. David declared: *"Bless the Lord, O my soul: and all that is within me, bless His holy name. Bless the Lord, O my soul, and forget not all His benefits: who forgiveth all thine iniquities; who healeth all thy diseases"* (Ps. 103:1-3). David says *forgives all* and *heals all* in the same breath.

Dr. John G. Lake wrote the following concerning the fact that divine healing is not something that is separate from the salvation that Christ came to bring:

> One of the difficulties concerning healing that God has to remove from the human mind is this wretched thing that often prevails in the best of Christian circles—that divine healing is something disassociated or separate from Christ's salvation. It is not. Healing is simply the salvation of Jesus Christ having its divine action in one's body, the same as it had its divine action in one's spirit. [1]

Healing Is Not Separate From Salvation

Within the Church, the major emphasis in our preaching and teaching has been placed upon the greatest miracle in the world—God's provision for the forgiveness of our sins. There are many who act on God's promises to receive forgiveness and cleansing of sin but do not as easily receive God's provision of healing for their body. They fail to understand that divine healing and forgiveness are both parts of the salvation that God has provided for through Christ.

The healing of the physical body is not something that is separate from salvation but is included in the Atonement. The divine flow of God's Spirit that liberates people from their sins, sets the drug addict free, and transforms the life of a hardened sinner to a child of the living God is the same divine *flow* of God's Spirit that destroys sickness and disease and heals a person's body.

God's purpose for sending Christ was not only to deliver humankind from satan's bondage and forgive their sins, but it was also to heal sicknesses and diseases of their physical body. Jesus came to *"destroy the works of the devil"* (1 John 3:8), whose works also include sickness and death. He did not come to bring a partial deliverance—to forgive you of your sins and deliver you out of the bondage of sin, but leave your body in bondage to sickness and disease, afflicted and tormented by satan. The power and anointing that flowed from Jesus broke every yoke of bondage upon humankind!

The *Same* Divine Flow of God's Spirit That Saves Also Heals!

One day, four men brought a man (sick of the palsy) to Jesus to be healed. Unable to get near Jesus because of the people pressing in to touch Him, they uncovered the roof and let his bed down through the roof. Notice Jesus' reaction. *"When Jesus saw their faith, He said unto the sick of the palsy, Son, thy sins be forgiven thee"* (Mark 2:5).

When some of the scribes sitting there heard Jesus, they began to question within themselves, *"Why does this man speak that way? He is blaspheming; who can forgive sins but God alone?"* (Mark 2:7 NASB). Jesus discerned what they were reasoning in their hearts and responded:

> *"Why are you reasoning about these things in your hearts? Which is easier, to say to the paralytic, 'Your sins are forgiven'; or to say, 'Get up, and pick up your pallet and walk'? But so that you may know that the Son of Man has authority on earth to forgive sins"—He said to the paralytic, "I say to you, get up, pick up your pallet and go home"* (Mark 2:8-11 NASB).

Jesus knew that the man needed to be healed of his paralyzed condition, but He first ministered to the man's soul. He also wanted the Pharisees and doctors of the law to know that He had been given power on earth to forgive men of their sins. He said, *"But so that you may know that the Son of Man has authority on earth to forgive sins"* (Mark 2:10 NASB), and He healed the man.

The man was immediately healed! He got up, picked up his bed, and walked out of the room.

Jesus Brought a Twofold Deliverance!

In this story, we can clearly see that Jesus came to bring a twofold deliverance: salvation and forgiveness of our sins and healing for our body. Forgiveness of sins and healing of the body go hand in hand. The same divine power that flows through Him to forgive our sins is there to heal our body. Jesus told the Pharisees, *"Which is easier, to say to the paralytic, 'Your sins are for-given'; or to say, 'Get up, and pick up your pallet and walk'?* (Mark 2:9 NASB). The words "saved," "healed," and "made whole" are all translated from the same Greek word, *sozo. Sozo* means, "to save," "to make well," "to heal," "to restore to health," "to deliver from the penal-ties of judgment." The word *sozo* carries the meaning of physical and spiritual healing. It is the same word that Jesus used when He said to the leper: *"Thy faith hath made thee whole [sozo]"* (Luke 17:19). It is also the word used in Luke 8:36: *"He that was possessed of the devils was healed [sozo]."*

According to Webster's Dictionary, *salvation* is "deliverance from sin and sin's penalty." A major part of that penalty is sickness. (Read Deuteronomy 28:15-61.) The word *salvation* is translated from the Greek word *soteria*, which implies deliverance, preservation, healing, health, and soundness. In the New Testament it is applied sometimes to the soul, and at other times, to the body only.

Salvation is full deliverance—Total Healing—spiritually, mentally, and physically. Both the Greek words for salvation and saved refer to spiritual *and* physical healing.

Recognize Christ As the Savior of Your Body, As Well As Your Soul

When you truly understand this truth, it will enable you to believe Christ for your healing, as well as for your salvation. As you received the salvation of your soul by faith, you can reach out by faith, and receive healing for your body. It does not take a greater faith to believe God for your healing than it does to believe Him for salvation.

Praise God, we serve an unlimited God. He forgives all of our iniquities and heals all of our diseases! The same divine power that flowed through Christ to heal this man's paralyzed body was released to cleanse him and forgive him of his sins.

You must recognize that Christ is the Savior of your body, as well as your soul. Act in faith to claim His miraculous provision for your healing, as well as for all of your other needs!

―――――◄○►―――――

Release Your Faith Now, and Claim Psalm 103:2-3. It Is Part of God's Contract for Your Healing.

Bless the Lord, O my soul, and forget not all His benefits: who forgiveth all thine iniquities; who healeth all thy diseases (Psalm 103:2-3).

―――――◄○►―――――

Make the Following Confession of Your Faith Throughout the Day:

Through Christ, God has provided total healing for every area of my life. He has delivered me out of all bondages of the enemy, including sin, sickness, and disease. By faith, I claim total healing now. He forgives all of my iniquities and heals all of my diseases!

Endnote

1. Dr. John G. Lake, The John G. Lake Sermons on Dominion Over Demons, Disease and Death, Christ for the Nations, Dallas, TX, Reprint 2007.

Day 13

HEALING PROVISION #6

*And the prayer of faith shall save the sick, and
the Lord shall raise him up* (James 5:15).

Scripture Reading: James 5:13-18

We have the assurance from God's Word that the
prayer of faith *will* save the sick. James didn't say that
they *might* be healed. He said that when the prayer of
faith is offered, it *will* save the sick, and the Lord *will*
raise him up!

Prayer doesn't save the sick. The ***prayer of faith*** saves
the sick!

A person may pray for hours, weeks, days, or months
for healing, but unless faith is released with their
prayers, the praying alone will not produce results.

Wesley Duewel said, "Hours and hours of praying do not eliminate the need for faith. They may help you to arrive at the position of faith, but without the dynamic of faith, prayer does not prevail."

The Prayer Command of Faith

When Jesus was among the people, He did not pray for the sick. There is only one recorded instance of Jesus openly calling upon the Father before healing someone. He did not pray a long, drawn-out prayer. He was not begging and pleading with God to heal the sick or meet the needs of the people. He didn't pray, *If* it be your will, heal. He *knew* that it was His Father's will to heal the sick because God had anointed Him and sent Him to destroy the works of the devil!

Jesus spent time alone with God in prayer, but when He ministered to the people, He spoke the prayer command of faith, and the work was accomplished. When He spoke, the power of God was released; and whatever He spoke came to pass. He spoke to the impossible circumstances in people's lives, and their lives were changed, healed, delivered, and set free!

- To the leper, Jesus spoke the prayer command of faith.

- He commanded, *Be clean,* and immediately the leper was cleansed and made whole.

- To the woman who had been bowed over with a spirit of infirmity for 18 years, Jesus spoke the prayer command of faith: *"Woman, thou art loosed from thine infirmity. And He laid His hands on her: and immediately she was made straight, and glorified God"* (Luke 13:12-13).

- Jesus spoke to the blind beggar: *"Receive thy sight.... And immediately he received his sight"* (Luke 18:42-43).

- To the widow's son, who had died and was being carried away to be buried, Jesus spoke the prayer command of faith: *"Young man, I say unto thee, Arise. And he that was dead sat up, and began to speak"* (Luke 7:14-15).

- Apostle Paul saw a man who had been crippled since birth. He spoke the prayer command of faith: *"Stand up on your feet!"* (Acts 14:10 NIV), and the man was instantly healed.

- Peter said to the lame man, who was lying at the gate of the temple: *"In the name of Jesus Christ of Nazareth rise up and walk. And he took him by the right hand, and lifted him up: and immediately his feet and ankle bones received strength.*

And he leaping up stood, and walked, and entered with them into the temple, walking, and leaping, and praising God" (Acts 3:6-8).

Prayer Without Faith Is Powerless

One of the reasons we are not living in this powerful dimension of prayer (where we are able to speak the prayer command of faith, and see blind eyes opened, the deaf hear, and the lame walk) is that we have not first shut ourselves in with the Father to receive His direction and draw upon His strength.

As a result, our faith is weak.

Faith is the one ingredient that we must have in our prayers. We know that without faith, it is impossible to please God (see Heb. 11:6). If you are not coming before the Father believing that He is a Rewarder and that He will give you what you are asking for when you bring Him your petitions, then don't waste your breath! If you are going to live in the same powerful dimension of prayer that Christ demonstrated, then you must live in the Spirit, and ***pray in faith!***

Christ lived and operated in a powerful dimension of prayer. His eyes were not focused upon the circumstances and situations in the natural world but upon the invisible, eternal, Almighty God, with whom nothing is impossible! To pray the prayer of faith for healing, you must pray with your spiritual focus set and your faith firmly fixed upon a faithful God who has bound Himself to you with His Word. Believe that He will answer your prayer.

Believe That You Receive Your Healing *When* You Pray!

There is no way that an individual can pray the prayer of faith for their healing if they are not fully convinced, according to the Word of God, that it is His will to heal them. When you pray, your faith must be based on the solid foundation of knowing God's contract of healing for you. There is not one example that is given to you in the Word of God where you are taught to pray, *If* it be your will, *please* heal me. Not one! When you go to Christ for your healing, you must first know that He has made full provision for your healing and that it is His will to heal you.

Your faith must not waver. You must continue to expect and believe that God will heal you, regardless of whether or not you see a physical manifestation. When you pray for healing, if you don't believe you have received it, you won't receive it. Jesus said: *"What things so ever ye desire, when ye pray, believe that ye receive them, and ye shall have them"* (Mark 11:24).

Regardless of the circumstances—the symptoms— the pain—you must not be moved. Continue to claim your healing. When your faith is being tested and tried, you must continue to believe, and act in faith. Know that the work has been done!

Speak the Prayer Command of Faith. Command Sickness and Disease to *Go*, in Jesus' Name!

Christ wants you to live in the same powerful dimension of prayer that He demonstrated throughout His life. He expects you to believe Him for the impossible. He wants you to pray with faith. Believe and know that He will change the very course of nature, if necessary, to answer your prayers.

When you pray the prayer command of faith, you take your position with Christ on the throne. You speak into your circumstances with all of Heaven backing you up. You speak in the power and authority of Jesus' name, as Christ spoke with the power and authority of the Father's name and backing.

You speak the prayer command of faith, in Jesus' name, and command the spirits of infirmity and disease to leave your body.

Knowing that it is God's will for you to be healed, speak the prayer command of faith to arthritis, heart disease, diabetes, high blood pressure, cancer, growths, tumors, and every other sickness and disease.

Command them to go, in Jesus' name! As you speak healing to your body, believe that you have received your healing. Put your faith into action. Receive your healing by faith, and praise Him for it!

Continue to stand, and act in faith upon the Word. Speak forth God's promises. Know that the work has been done!

Claim James 5:15. It Is a Provision of God's Contract for Your Healing.

> *And the prayer of faith shall save the sick, and the Lord shall raise him up; and if he have committed sins, they shall be forgiven him* (James 5:15).

Make the Following Your Confession of Faith Throughout the Day:

> *The prayer of faith will save the sick! I claim God's provision of healing for my body. I command the spirit of infirmity and all sicknesses and diseases to leave my body now! I receive total healing of every cell, organ, and tissue in my body. I command them to function normally and to come into alignment with God's Word and provision for divine healing!*

Day 14

HEALING PROVISION #7

And these signs shall follow them that believe;
in My name shall they cast out devils; they shall
speak with new tongues...they shall lay hands
on the sick, and they shall recover
(Mark 16:17-18).

Scripture Reading: Luke 10:1-9; Acts 3:6-8 and 9:40-41

Jesus never intended for God's healing power to be released through Him alone. When He saw the great multitudes following Him—the broken, diseased bodies and those being tormented by demons—He was moved with compassion. He called His disciples together and gave them power and authority to preach, cast out devils, and heal all types of sicknesses and diseases. *"And when He had called unto Him His twelve disciples, He gave them power against unclean spirits, to cast them out, and to heal all manner of sickness and all manner of disease"* (Matt. 10:1).

Once again, we see God's plan and provision for healing revealed. As He sent the disciples forth into the cities, Jesus told them: *"As ye go, preach, saying, The kingdom of heaven is at hand. Heal the sick, cleanse the lepers, raise the dead, cast out devils: freely ye have received, freely give"* (Matt. 10:7-8).

Healing is part of the Kingdom of Heaven. Christ came to bring healing to this world, and He intended for His disciples and followers to have the same power to heal the sick that He had.

We read that a flow of God's healing power was released through the disciples as they went through the towns within Judea and Samaria.

> *And they departed, and went through the towns, preaching the gospel, and healing every where* (Luke 9:6).

> *And they cast out many devils, and anointed with oil many that were sick, and healed them* (Mark 6:13).

Christ Intends for God's HealingPower to Flow—Unhindered—Through His Church

Before He ascended into Heaven, Christ commissioned His disciples. He told them that He was going to send the Holy Spirit to give them the power to do the same works that He had done.

He said:

> *He that believeth on Me, the works that I do shall he do also; and greater works than these shall he do; because I go unto My Father....And I will pray the Father, and He shall give you another Comforter, that He may abide with you for ever* (John 14:12,16).

After the Day of Pentecost (when the Holy Spirit came with power and fire upon the believers), God's healing power was manifested through the believers wherever they went. As they spoke the Word and laid hands on the sick, demons were cast out, sicknesses and diseases were healed, the lame walked, and the dead were raised!

A multitude of people from surrounding cities brought the sick, diseased, and demon-possessed to Jerusalem, and ***they were all healed!***

...They brought forth the sick into the streets, and laid them on beds and couches, that at the least the shadow of Peter passing by might overshadow some of them. There came also a multitude out of the cities round about unto Jerusalem, bringing sick folks, and them which were vexed with unclean spirits: and they were healed every one (Acts 5:15-16).

This is a picture of what Christ intends for the Church to be today—a healing center, where suffering humanity can come to be healed and delivered from the oppression of satan!

The same healing power that flowed through Jesus was released through the Early Church, in the power and authority of His name. Healing was not just released through the ministry of the apostles but also through the other *believers.* Jesus said: *"And these signs shall follow them that believe; in My name shall they cast out devils; they shall speak with new tongues...they shall lay hands on the sick, and they shall recover"* (Mark 16:17-18).

Christ Intends for You to Heal the Sick!

Let these Scriptures go deep into your spirit. Regardless of those who have taught that healing is no longer for today or that miracles have ceased, Christ intends for *every believer*—through the power and authority of the Holy Spirit—to lay hands on the sick and see them recover. You may have read these Scriptures many times but have not acted in faith upon them because you have thought that ministering to the sick was the work of evangelists, pastors, or others of the fivefold ministry. You may have thought that praying for the sick was only for those who had great faith and that you didn't have enough faith.

Jesus said, *"He that believeth on Me, the works that I do shall he do also; and greater works than these shall he do; because I go unto My Father"* (John 14:12). Are you a child of God? Do you believe Christ's promise that you will do the same works that He did and greater than He did?

Are you ready to receive your healing and be used by God to lay hands on the sick, and see them healed by His almighty power?

Use the Power and Authority That He Has Given to You in His Name!

Jesus has appointed you to be His legal representative, to act in His place and on His behalf. While He was here on this earth, He healed the sick in the power and authority of His Father's name. On Resurrection Day, He broke the power of sin, sickness, and death. He ascended into Heaven and gave you the full power and authority to use His name—to act in His place—*to heal the sick!*

Sicknesses and diseases are the works of the enemy. You don't need to pray to determine whether or not it is God's will to heal the sick. Jesus paid the price. The war has been won. He has destroyed the power of sickness. He has authorized you to heal the sick in the power and authority of His name.

Wherever you see people bound by sickness, claim Mark 16:17-18, and lay hands on them. In the name of Jesus, rebuke and take authority over spirits of infirmity, blind, deaf, and dumb spirits, and command them to go. As you use the name of Jesus, remember that all He is and all of the power that He has today is in His name! The power and authority to do the same mighty works that Jesus did is in His name. It legally belongs to you, but unless you reach out by faith, take it, and use it, that power will never be realized in your life.

———◄○►———

Claim Mark 16:17-18 as Part of God's Contract for Your Healing Today!

And these signs shall follow them that believe; in My name shall they cast out devils; they shall speak with new tongues...they shall lay hands on the sick, and they shall recover (Mark 16:17-18).

Face your sicknesses and physical problems and those of your loved ones and people around you in the power and authority that Christ has given to you in His name. Claim your healing. Speak the word of healing over your body. Lay hands on those who need healing. Expect and believe that God's healing power will be released, in Jesus' name!

———◄o►———

Make the Following Your Confession of Faith, and Repeat It Throughout the Day:

Jesus promised that signs and wonders will follow me. He has given me the power and authority to heal the sick in His name. I claim this promise and believe that as I lay hands on the sick, they will be healed and delivered by God's healing power.

Part III

Your Seven-Point Strategy to Defeat Satan's Attacks Against Your Physical Body

Day 15

STRATEGY #1: REFUSE TO ACCEPT YOUR SYMPTOMS OR THE DOCTOR'S REPORT AS THE FINAL WORD!

And these signs shall follow them that believe;
in My name shall they cast out devils; they shall
speak with new tongues…they shall lay hands
on the sick, and they shall recover
(Mark 16:17-18).

Scripture Reading: Hebrews 6:13-19, First Kings 8:56, and Isaiah 55:11

God has given you His contract—His unchangeable, infallible, and impregnable Word, which cannot fail and will never pass away. Remember: *"God is not a man, that He should lie; neither the son of man, that He should repent: hath He said, and shall He not do it? or hath He spoken, and shall He not make it good?"* (Num. 23:19). He has promised: *"My covenant will I not break, nor alter the thing that is gone out of My lips"* (Ps. 89:34).

Once again, we see God's plan and provision for healing revealed. As He sent the disciples forth into the cities, Jesus told them: *"As ye go, preach, saying, The kingdom of heaven is at hand. Heal the sick, cleanse the lepers, raise the dead, cast out devils: freely ye have received, freely give"* (Matt. 10:7-8).

The only way that this contract for your healing can become effective is for you to sign your name to it! A contract becomes effective only when it is signed by all involved parties.

God has given you this contract (with its provisions for your healing), which has been signed and sealed by the blood of Jesus. You must believe it, and sign your name to it by acting upon it. You must claim every one of its promises, and act in faith upon them before it will become effective, before you will experience a release of God's healing power in your life.

Once you know what is in God's contract for your healing, you will be able to believe God, and release your faith to receive healing. You will also be able to resist satan's attempts to put sickness upon your body, and believe God to *keep* sicknesses and diseases away from you!

Don't Accept Your Symptoms or the Doctor's Report as the Final Word!

You know that Christ has given you a contract that provides for your healing. Use this knowledge to break through satan's sevenfold attack against your body! Don't you dare sit there and allow satan to put sickness upon your body!

When you first feel any signs or symptoms of disease, or hear the doctor's report that you have a serious disease, or that someone you love has been afflicted with an incurable disease, don't accept it as the final word. Satan is a liar! Don't listen to him! Thank God for the medical help that is available. Respect it, but remember that humankind does not have the final word.

God's Word—not the doctor's report or the symptoms of your disease—is the final word!

You know that Christ took your sicknesses and diseases upon Himself. He has lifted (removed!) them from you. He has broken the power of sin, sickness, and death over your life. Because of these truths, you can boldly rebuke satan with the Word of God, and he must flee!

You know that satan cannot lay a disease upon your body because Christ has already borne your diseases. When symptoms of sickness or disease try to take hold in your body, do not fear them. Reject them! Through the power and authority of the Holy Spirit, get satan on his side of the line!

Regardless of Your Pain, Stay Focused on God and His Promises

The most difficult time to remain determined that God will heal you is in the midst of enduring physical pain.

I understand what pain is.

There have been times when God has allowed me to feel excruciating pain for a reason and a purpose. I have also felt the sting of tremendous emotional pain.

However, I also know that in the midst of pain, God can steady our spirit and mind and give us the ability to hold on to the hand of Jesus to receive our healing.

The Miraculous Healing of My Jawbone

When I was just a young man, my jawbone was broken in a baseball game. The doctor told me that he would need to order a special brace from New Jersey to hold my jaw properly in place. He said that I would need to wear this brace for at least six months.

Until the brace arrived, he wrapped an elastic cloth band tightly around my head to lock my jaw into place. I was unable to eat, except for what I could get through a plastic straw.

I had made a commitment to preach in an upstate New York, little Pentecostal church. Now, under these circumstances, everyone expected me to cancel the invitation. In fact, I did cancel, but one day, during prayer in my room at school, God spoke to my heart. He told me that if I would keep the invitation, He would heal me. I told my friends and fellow students that I was going to keep the speaking engagement and that God was going to heal me.

Sometimes, it's not good to reveal everything that God tells you, unless you are prepared to pass through an awful period of criticism and unbelief until it comes to pass.

The week prior to the meeting, everyone was on pins and needles, wondering whether this crazy, young man, named *Morris,* was going to bring a terrible disgrace on the school. I was expecting to have a small crowd of 10 to 15 people, but when it was time for the service to begin, the place was packed. There were about a hundred people. It seemed as if the entire student body was there!

Faith and Obedience Are Major Keys to Your Healing!

In obedience to the Word that God gave me to go, be faithful, and preach because He would heal me, I walked up the steps of the church and tore off the binding that had been holding my jaw in place. My jaw dropped. The pain was so excruciating that it was enough to cause four or five people to pass out; yet, I refused to keep my eyes on my physical condition.

With my jaw hanging down, I entered the church, walked down the aisle, and took my seat on the platform. There I sat. I couldn't speak. I couldn't sing—nothing.

With every eye upon me, anxiously waiting to see what was going to transpire, I stepped up to the platform. The moment that I opened my mouth to read the Bible, a miracle took place in front of that congregation. My jaw miraculously snapped back into place! The bones were instantly healed, and I preached my entire message that night without a problem.

Don't Give Up!

In that little, white church in New York, a young, 17-year-old boy, named *Morris,* saw God as He is: a loving Father anxiously waiting to meet me at the point of my need.

I saw a God who is unlimited and all powerful.

I saw beyond the natural limitations of my broken jaw and experienced the release of a supernatural manifestation of God's healing power to heal me—and so can you!

There are many times when you may not feel that you can endure the pain and feel like giving up.

Don't give up!

Whether or not you are in pain, God is still God. His Word and His promises of healing are true, regardless of your physical condition or pain.

In his book, *Healing the Sick*, T.L. Osborn states the following concerning accepting symptoms and confessing sickness:

> *Confessing pains, aches, and diseases is like signing for a package that the post office has delivered. Satan then has the receipt—your confession—from you, showing that you have accepted his package. Do not accept anything sent by the devil. Even though your five senses may testify that it has come to you, refuse to confess it. Look immediately to the Word of God. Remember, you were healed!*[1]

Reject every doubt, every thought, every action, and every word that does not line up with God's Word.

Continually speak forth God's Word in faith. Confess His promises of healing. Act on them. As you do, God's healing power will be released, and it will destroy the disease in your body.

Instead of acknowledging and talking about your symptoms, act in faith on God's contract of healing.

————◄○►————

Make the Following Declaration of Your Faith, Based on Galatians 3:13 and First Peter 2:24:

Christ has redeemed me from the curse and its consequences, including sicknesses and diseases. Through His blood, I am set free from the powers of sin, sickness, and death. On the cross, Jesus took my sins and sicknesses upon Himself. With His stripes, I was healed—past tense!

Endnote

1. T.L. Osborn, *Healing the Sick* (Osborn International, 1992).

Day 16

STRATEGY #2: ACT ON GOD'S WORD!

Scripture Reading: Matthew 8:5-13

Knowing that one of satan's strategies is to wear down your spiritual and physical resistance by hitting you hard with one sickness after another, saturate and cover yourself with God's Word.

You have a choice. You can take hold of God's contract, claim His healing provisions, and take a step of faith by acting on His Word; or, you can keep your eyes on your symptoms, listen to the lies of the enemy, and remain sick.

Regardless of What You May Think:

I've had this sickness for such a long time. I don't think I have enough faith to believe. I've tried to believe in the past for my healing, but I'm still not healed.

Regardless of What You See:

The obvious physical manifestations of my sickness—crippled hands and/or feet, paralyzed legs, muscle deterioration, swelling in the joints, evidence of heart or liver disease, and the physical problems associated with diabetes or other long-term illnesses.

Regardless of What You Hear:

"You have an incurable disease. There's nothing that we can do to help you. You will just have to learn to live with your sickness or disability."

Regardless of What You Feel:

Pain, fear, discouragement, defeat, or hopelessness.

God has given you the promises in His Word that will bring healing and deliverance from all sickness and disease. There is absolutely nothing too hard for Him! God is saying to you: *"Behold, I am the Lord, the God of all flesh: is there any thing too hard for Me?"* (Jer. 32:27).

God's Word Possesses the Power for Its Own Fulfillment!

Once you understand that the power that created the heavens and the earth—the sun, moon, stars, animals, and every living thing—is the same power that is contained in every promise that God has given to you, you will realize that God's Word is the most powerful force upon the earth today. Its power is not limited by any circumstance that you may face.

It is impossible to separate God and His Word. They are one. All that can be said about God can be said about His Word.

God is all-powerful—so is His Word.

God is holy—so is His Word.

God is faithful—so is His Word.

God is unchanging—so is His Word.

God is all-knowing—so is His Word.

God cannot fail—neither can His Word.

God is everlasting—so is His Word.

Faith and Power Are in the Word!

God's Word is not vulnerable. He is not depending upon a faith that you can somehow develop. He is not depending upon whether or not you can demonstrate enough super faith to produce a miracle. God's Word remains true, regardless of whether or not some do not believe. *"For what if some did not believe? shall their unbelief make the faith of God without effect? God forbid: yea, let God be true, but every man a liar"* (Rom. 3:3-4).

As you act on the Word and are faithful to speak it forth, it will be done! Jesus said, *"If you have faith as small as a mustard seed, you can say to this mountain, 'Move from here to there' and it will move. Nothing will be impossible for you"* (Matt. 17:20 NIV).

Christ has planned for you to speak to the mountains (the impossible situations)—the mountain of your sickness, the mountain of your financial needs, the mountain of your family problems—and see them removed. He said that even if you only have faith as small as the grain of a tiny mustard seed, you will be able to do it!

Remember, you cannot separate God from His Word. The power for the fulfillment of His Word is not in any human or in anything a person possesses. The power for the fulfillment of that Word is in the Word itself.

God sent His Word *"and healed them"* (Ps. 107:20).

God promised:

> *So shall My word be that goes forth out of My mouth: it shall not return to Me void [without producing any effect, useless], but it shall accomplish that which I please and purpose, and it shall prosper in the thing for which I sent it* (Isaiah 55:11 AMP).

Jesus, the Living Word, came to *"destroy the works of the devil"* (1 John 3:8).

Jesus' Words Were Pregnant With the Life of God!

As Jesus spoke the words that the Father had given Him to speak, He did not one time doubt or wonder if what He spoke would come to pass. He knew that He was speaking forth the words of Almighty God, Jehovah, who said: *"Let there be light: and there was light"* (Gen. 1:3). He knew that God's Word was all-powerful and would come to pass!

The evil spirits were powerless before Jesus. With just one Word from His lips, He cast them out! Jesus told His disciples: *"The words that I speak unto you, they are spirit, and they are life"* (John 6:63). The very words coming forth from His mouth were given to Him from God, and they were alive. Within them were the power to bring them to pass. Within His words were eternal life, healing, deliverance—all that God originally purposed for man to enjoy upon this earth.

As Jesus taught on the hillside and in the synagogues, the people *"...were astonished at His doctrine: for His word was with power"* (Luke 4:32). As He spoke the Word—blind eyes were opened, demons were cast out, and the dead were raised.

Through the power and authority of the Holy Spirit, the believers in the Early Church spoke the Word, and witnessed the same results. Through the power and anointing of the Holy Spirit, God has planned for you to do the same!

Christ Intends for You to Speak the Word, and See the Same Results!

Speaking or confessing the Word is more than memorizing and repeating certain Scriptures. It is not based upon following a specific formula or man-made doctrine. We must have a confession of faith, but it is more than just being able to use our lips to confess the Word. We must use our lips to confess the words that are anointed with the power that comes from experience— that comes from a revelation of the Word. It involves not only speaking or confessing the written Word of God, but also speaking the words that the Holy Spirit directs us to speak. We speak the words of healing and deliverance in Jesus' name, under the anointing of the Holy Spirit, as the believers did in the Early Church.

Regardless of who you are or how insignificant you may feel, when you come into that spiritual union with Christ—when you know that He is in you, and you are in Him—you will be able to act in faith, and speak forth His Word in power. You will not doubt or waver because you will know that as you face satan's power, the living Word is speaking through you, and satan must obey. The key to your victory is in your union with Him. Jesus said, *"If ye abide in Me, and My words abide in you, ye shall ask what ye will, and it shall be done unto you"* (John 15:7).

Focus upon your needs. You may have physical problems and sickness in your body—diabetes, high blood pressure, stomach trouble, back problems, bladder conditions, deaf ears—whatever the need, focus on it right now.

The power of God is in the Word to meet you at the point of your need and heal you.

God has placed the living Word in you. He has placed the written Word in your heart and in your mouth. Let it come forth like a mighty, healing stream! Take hold of God's contract for your healing, and act on His Word. Take authority over the spirits of infirmity and disease that are afflicting your body, and command them to go, in Jesus' name!

————◄○►————

In the Power and Anointing of the Holy Spirit, Speak God's Word of Healing and Deliverance Over Your Body:

God has promised that His Word shall not return unto Him void, but it shall accomplish its purpose. According to His promises in First Peter 2:24 and Isaiah 53:5, I speak life and healing into every cell of my body. In the name of Jesus, I command all sickness and disease to leave my body. My body is the temple of the Holy Spirit. No sickness or disease can remain! God's healing power is flowing through me to restore health to my body.

Day 17

STRATEGY #3: BOLDLY REBUKE SATAN!

Scripture Reading: Luke 4:32-39

As Jesus began to teach and minister to the needs of the people, He was so full of the Holy Spirit, and His words were so full of power, that the people were amazed. *"And they were all amazed, and spake among themselves, saying, What a word is this! for with authority and power He commandeth the unclean spirits, and they come out"* (Luke 4:36).

The English word *authority* in the above Scripture is the Greek word *exousia,* which means, "the right to exercise power." The word *power* in the Greek translation is *dunamis,* which refers to the supernatural, miracle-working power of God. Jesus was given the authority (*exousia,* the right to exercise power) to use

God's power (*dunamis,* the miracle-working power of God) through the Holy Spirit. Knowing that He had been anointed with the Holy Spirit and with power, He confronted satan and immediately took action.

Evil Spirits Had to Obey Him!

The evil spirits also recognized who Jesus was and were afraid. One day while He was teaching in the synagogue, a man with an unclean spirit saw Jesus and cried out: *"Ah, let us alone! What have You to do with us [What have we in common], Jesus of Nazareth? Have You come to destroy us? I know Who You are—the Holy One of God!"* (Luke 4:34 AMP).

Jesus was not intimidated by the presence of these evil spirits. He didn't hesitate. He spoke directly to the unclean spirit: *"But Jesus rebuked him, saying, Be silent (muzzled, gagged), and come out of him! And when the demon had thrown the man down in their midst, he came out of him, without injuring him in any possible way"* (Luke 4:35 AMP).

Evil spirits were subject to His Word. They had to obey Him!

Rebuke Means, "Stop! You Can't Go Any Farther!"

The word *rebuke* in Luke 4:35 is taken from the Greek word *epitimao,* which means "to censure," "to

forbid," "to charge," and "to rebuke."[1] This word sig-
nifies much more than just a simple reprimand. Jesus
wasn't just saying to this demon, "Now, you know you
shouldn't be tormenting this poor man. Why don't you
leave him alone?"

By Jesus rebuking this demon, He was taking
authority over him and commanding him to go! He
was forbidding the demon from controlling the man.
He was demanding him to get his hands off, and keep
them off, this man's life!

To *rebuke* simply means, "Stop," "That's enough,"
"You've gone far enough," "You can't go any farther"!

With this same power and authority, Jesus rebuked
sickness. One day, Jesus came to Simon's house and
found Simon's mother-in-law sick with a raging fever.
*"And He stood over her, and rebuked the fever; and it left her:
and immediately she arose and ministered unto them"* (Luke
4:39). Jesus rebuked the fever. He commanded it to go,
and it obeyed!

After the father brought his boy to Jesus' disciples,
and they were unable to cast out the unclean spirit that
was tormenting the boy, the disciples brought him to
Jesus. The evil spirit recognized Jesus and immediately
threw the boy into a convulsion. He fell to the ground
and began rolling about and foaming at the mouth.
Jesus immediately recognized the work of the enemy.
He knew the power and authority that had been given

to Him, and He spoke directly to the unclean spirit. He rebuked him, saying, *"You deaf and mute spirit, I command you, come out of him and do not enter him again"* (Mark 9:25 NASB).

Rebuke Satan, and Command Him to Stop!

When you know that Christ has borne your infirmities and sicknesses, you can resist satan and his lying symptoms of disease. You have no fear. You boldly *rebuke* satan, in the name of Jesus.

Through the anointing of the Holy Spirit, God has given you the same power to rebuke, command, and take authority over and defeat satan and every demonic power in all of the circumstances in your life! Christ promised: *"But ye shall receive power, after that the Holy Ghost has come upon you..."* (Acts 1:8). The power referred to in this verse is the *same dunamis,* miracle-working power that was manifested in Jesus' life.

You have been given power and authority over all of the power of the enemy. Jesus said:

> *Behold! I have given you authority and power to trample upon serpents and scorpions, and [physical and mental strength and ability] over all the*

power that the enemy [possesses]; and nothing shall
in any way harm you (Luke 10:19 AMP).

Through the Holy Spirit, you have authority (*exou-sia*, "the right to exercise power") and power (*dunamis*, "the miracle-working power of God") to rebuke satan, the spirit of infirmity, and all of the foul spirits attacking your body with sickness and disease. Command them, as Jesus did, to go![2]

Don't Be Afraid to Speak Directly to Satan or the Spirits of Infirmity That Are Afflicting You

God does not intend for you to try to face the onslaught of the enemy attacking your body in the power of your own limited strength. He has planned for you to be able to look satan right in the face, and (with the same power and authority that Jesus had) command him, Stop! That's enough! You've gone far enough! You can't go any farther! Get out, and stay out!

Don't be afraid to speak to satan, to the spirit of infirmity, to unclean spirits, or the foul, tormenting spirits that are attacking you and your loved ones. Jesus spoke directly to evil spirits. In the synagogue in Capernaum, Jesus rebuked the unclean spirit in a man. He said, *"Hold thy peace, and come out of him"* (Luke 4:35). He rebuked the dumb and deaf spirit in a young man who had been brought to Him. He spoke directly to the dumb and deaf spirit: *"Thou dumb and deaf spirit, I charge thee, come out of him, and enter no more into him"* (Mark 9:25).

Ask God to reveal to you the spirits that are afflicting your body. Then, in the name of Jesus, begin to rebuke—command—satan and the spirits of infirmity to stop attacking your body, to loose their hold, and leave your body!

————◄○►————

Through the Power of the Holy Spirit, You Have Been Given the Power and Authority Over All of the Power of the Enemy. Exercise It by Rebuking the Unclean Spirits That Are Attacking Your Body:

> *Satan, in the power and authority that Christ has given to me over all of your power, I rebuke you and every spirit of infirmity that is afflicting my body. I command you to stop! Leave my body now, in the name of Jesus! Christ has broken the power of sin, sickness, and death. You cannot afflict my body any longer! By the stripes that Jesus took on His back for my healing, I am now healed and made whole, from the top of my head to the soles of my feet!*

Endnotes

1. http://www.searchgodsword.org.

2. Ibid.

Day 18

STRATEGY #4: REJECT SATAN'S LIES, AND GO TO THE ROOT CAUSE OF YOUR SICKNESS

Scripture Reading: Luke 13:10-17

Satan will lie to you and make you think that it is not God's will to heal you. Reject his lies!

Stand firm, and make your confession of faith based upon God's contract for your healing.

When the enemy tries to bind you or your loved ones with sickness and disease, instead of becoming fearful, go to the root cause. Command the spirit of infirmity to loose its hold and leave your body, in Jesus' name!

When you attack the root cause of the sickness or disease that is afflicting your body, it is vitally important for you to understand that sickness is a result of sin that came upon humankind because of Adam's and Eve's disobedience in the Garden of Eden. It is part of the consequences of the curse. Satan is the source of sickness and disease.

You must have a revelation that satan's power over you is broken! Because you have been given power and authority over satan and his principalities (just as Christ has given you power over sin), you have the power and authority to rebuke satan, and command sickness to go, in Jesus' name!

The power and anointing that flowed from Jesus broke every yoke of bondage upon humankind! Look at Acts 10:38 again: *"God anointed Jesus of Nazareth with the Holy Ghost and with power: who went about doing good, and healing all that were oppressed of the devil; for God was with Him."* Jesus healed *all* who were oppressed by the devil!

Sickness: The Result of Unconfessed Sin

Some people are sick because of unconfessed sin in their life. Whenever there is unresolved anger, hatred, bitterness, unforgiveness, and other sins within a person's life—that they have not confessed and allowed Christ to cleanse them from—it is an open door for sickness or infirmity to come upon them. However, when they confess these things, and get rid of them, they will be healed.

As you pray and believe God for your healing, ask Him to reveal if there is any unforgiveness or unconfessed sin in your heart that may hinder you from being healed. Repent of any anger, hatred, bitterness, unforgiveness, or any other unconfessed sin in your life.

Sickness: The Result of Violating the Natural Laws of God

There are some sicknesses that result when a person violates the natural laws of God. A great majority of the sicknesses and diseases that are prevalent in the life of many people are the direct result of their failure to follow the basic guidelines of good nutrition, proper exercise, and general proper care for their body.

Stress-induced or stress-related diseases include tuberculosis, multiple sclerosis, leukemia, diabetes, and hypoglycemia. Stress affects the heart, wears down the immune system, and increases susceptibility to almost every other disease.

Your body is the temple of the Holy Spirit. If you are abusing it by failing to eat healthy foods, exercise, and take proper care of yourself, then how can you expect God to heal you?

What? know ye not that your body is the temple of the Holy Ghost which is in you, which ye have of God, and ye are not your own? For ye are bought with a price: therefore glorify God in your body, and in your spirit, which are God's (1 Corinthians 6:19-20).

If you have been careless and overeating, eating unhealthy foods, or failing to exercise and take care of your body, ask God to forgive you. Take steps to follow the basic guidelines of good nutrition. Get out and exercise. Determine to follow the biblical guidelines for healthy living.

It has been estimated by doctors that 60 percent of illnesses result from an unhealthy lifestyle. The Bible is filled with examples of following the natural laws of health for example when Paul told the men on the ship to eat for their health (see Acts 2:34). He told Timothy to drink wine instead of the bad water (see 1 Tim. 5:23). Chapter 11 of Leviticus contains God's instructions to the children of Israel concerning which animals were considered unclean and were not to eat.

The same God who said He is the God who heals you also gave practical dietary regulations as part of the Old Testament law. Your body, as well as your spirit, is sacred because it is the temple of God. Proper rest, exercise, and diet will help you to walk in divine health because you are cooperating with the natural laws of God. Because your body is the temple of the Holy Spirit, do not take any toxic substances into it, such as alcohol, cigarettes, or addictive drugs.

Sickness: The Result of Oppressing Spirits

As we study Jesus' ministry of healing, it is evident that there are many instances in which sickness is the direct result of oppressing spirits. Throughout His ministry, when He dealt with sickness, Jesus recognized that it was the work of satan.

In Luke chapter 13, we read that Jesus was teaching in the synagogue. There was a woman who was bowed together and could not straighten up. The Word says that she had had a spirit of infirmity for 18 long years. (Refer to Luke 13:11.) Today, doctors would diagnose her condition as crippling rheumatoid arthritis or some other disease affecting her spine. They would never consider the root cause to be a demonic spirit. The Word clearly states that her condition was the result of a spirit of infirmity.

Jesus stopped what He was doing and called her to Him. He spoke with power and authority: *"Woman, thou art loosed from thine infirmity"* (Luke 13:12). He laid His hands on her. Instantly she was made straight.

Jesus simply touched the woman and set her free. He made it clear that it was satan who had bound her. He told the leader of the synagogue (who had become angry because Jesus had healed her on the Sabbath): *"Ought not this woman, a daughter of Abraham, whom Satan has kept bound for eighteen years, be loosed from this bond on the Sabbath day?"* (Luke 13:16 AMP).

Go to the Root Cause of Sickness

Jesus didn't just deal with the symptoms or the sicknesses. He commanded the spirits that were oppressing the people to leave. Consider the following examples:

- A blind, mute man was brought to Jesus. When the devil was cast out, the man was able to see and speak. (See Matt. 12:22.)

- A mute man was brought to Jesus. When Jesus cast the devil out, the man was able to speak. (See Matt. 9:32.)

- Jesus cast the deaf and dumb spirits out of a boy. The boy was healed and could then hear and speak. (See Mark 9:25-27.)

- When Jesus healed a deaf man with a speech impediment, He spoke directly to the man's physical infirmity. He said, *"Be opened"* (Mark 7:34).

- Jesus spoke to the dead body of Jairus's daughter, commanded life to return to it, and she sat up. (See Mark 5:41.)

When you deal with sicknesses and diseases, you must never deal with them in the natural realm. You must understand that we are not in a natural conflict. Our battle is not against cancer, diabetes, high blood pressure, arthritis, and other diseases. We are in a spiritual warfare against the unclean spirits of infirmity that are the root cause of sickness.

Deal With Sickness and Disease the Way Jesus Did!

Instead of becoming fearful when the enemy tries to bind you or your loved ones with sickness and disease, rebuke it, in Jesus' name. Go to the root cause. Command the spirit of infirmity to loose its hold and leave your body. Jesus has destroyed the power of the curse and its resulting consequences.

Speak to the pain, disease, or infirmity. Command it to go!

Use the power and authority that Christ has given to you to bind the work of satan and the evil spirits that are attacking your body. Jesus said, *"Whatsoever thou shalt bind on earth shall be bound in heaven: and whatsoever thou shalt loose on earth shall be loosed in heaven"* (Matt. 16:19).

Regardless of your condition or the symptoms or pain in your body, continue to exercise power and authority over the sickness and disease. Believe that the work has been done, in Jesus' name.

Take authority over sickness and disease. Treat them like Jesus treated them! Speak to the pain and the symptoms. Command them to go! Speak to the tumors and growths, and in Jesus' name, command them to dry up! Curse the cancer cells at their very root, and command them to die! In Jesus' name, speak to your weakened heart muscles to receive strength, and be healed!

Regardless of what sickness, disease, or infirmity you may have, use the power and authority that Christ has given to you in Matthew 18:18 to bind the powers of darkness. Command them to go, in Jesus' name.

Day 19

STRATEGY #5: USE THE POWER AND AUTHORITY OF JESUS' NAME

Scripture Reading: Acts 3:1-16; John 14:13-14, 16:23-24, and 15:16; Mark 6:15-18

Without a doubt, one of the most powerful spiritual weapons that Christ has given to enable you to face and overcome every attack of satan against you is His name! His name is the ultimate weapon—the ultimate strategy—and is 100-percent effective! You have been given the name that is above every other name! His name is all-powerful, indestructible, and unchangeable. It cannot fail. Therefore, you cannot fail!

Through the power and authority of His name, you are able to bind the foul spirits that are afflicting your body. Speak to the pain, the disease, or the infirmity, and command it to go. You have the power and authority to speak to tumors, growths, and cancers. In the name of Jesus, curse the cancer cells, and command them to dry up.

Say aloud: There is no sickness or disease that can remain in my body when I know the power of Jesus' name and use it!

It is my prayer for you that God will give you a fresh revelation of the awesome power that resides in Jesus' name and how it is released when you speak it forth in faith to receive healing into all of your circumstances.

Receive a Fresh Revelation of the Power of Jesus' Name

Asking in the name of Jesus is much more than simply repeating the words *in the name of Jesus.* It is sad to say, but true, that the vast majority of Christians today are not living in the fullness of the power that Christ intended for them to have in His name. When they pray, they include the words, *in Jesus' name,* but there is no real revelation. They are not experiencing the release of power and the miraculous results that Christ intended for them to experience.

When you have a revelation, and you know, that you know, that you know what is behind His name, the authority that belongs to you, your legal right to use His name, and the power that resides in His name, you will no longer be merely praying. You will not be begging. You will be invoking—putting into operation—the power to bring about what you desire. There will be no question or doubt that it will be done.

When You Use Jesus' Name, You Put Into Operation the Power Behind His Name!

In Acts 3:6, Peter told the lame man: *"Such as I have give I thee: in the name of Jesus Christ of Nazareth rise up and walk."* He did not pray, plead, or ask.

Peter did not face this man's infirmity in his own strength or in his own name. He had a *revelation* of Jesus' name. Jesus had told them: *"Whatsoever ye shall ask the Father in My name, He will give it you"* (John 16:23). He did not face that lame man wondering whether or not he would be healed. There was absolutely no hesitation. He had no doubt whatsoever! He knew that when he invoked the name of Jesus, He was putting into operation the power that was in Jesus' name to manifest the healing.

Peter said: *"Such as I have give I thee."* Peter was referring to the power and authority that he had in Jesus' name to heal the sick. Jesus had told them: *"Freely ye have received, freely give"* (Matt. 10:8).

Peter seized the man by the hand and raised him to his feet. Immediately, the man's feet and ankles were strengthened. He began to walk, leap, and praise God. The people were amazed and most likely wondered how it was possible that an ordinary man would be able to heal the lame. They had seen Jesus perform many miracles, but they had also watched Jesus die. He was no longer there.

Miracle-Working Power Is Released in Jesus' Name

Peter clearly revealed to them how the man had been healed. He said:

> *The God of Abraham, Isaac and Jacob, the God of our fathers, has glorified His servant Jesus....And on the basis of faith in His name, it is the name of Jesus which has strengthened this man whom you see and know* (Acts 3:13,16 NASB).

Peter wanted them to know that it was not by his own power—but through the power and authority of Jesus' name—that brought healing to the paralyzed man. He said:

> *Be it known unto you all, and to all the people of Israel, that by the name of Jesus Christ of Nazareth, whom ye crucified, whom God raised from the dead,*

even by Him doth this man stand here before you whole (Acts 4:10).

What Has Happened to the Church?

When we take the mask off, we will see that the Church today is not manifesting the power and authority of Jesus' name the way that it was manifested in the Early Church.

Why not?

One reason is that most Christians are facing their circumstances and satan's attacks against them in their own strength, instead of facing them in Jesus' name. What do the majority of Christians do when satan puts sickness on their body? They lean on the arm of the flesh. They run to the medicine cabinet or call the doctor.

I don't have anything against doctors or medicine, but I believe that your trust should be in *Jehovah-rapha*, "the Lord, your Healer." (Read Exodus 15:26.) You should face your battle with sickness and disease in the power and authority of Jesus' name. The moment that you are attacked with a sickness, you must find someone to agree with you, and take authority over it, in Jesus' name.

There Is No Greater Name!

For a moment, think about the power that Christ possesses. He is seated at the right hand of the Father:

Far above all principality, and power, and might, and dominion, and every name that is named, not only in this world, but also in that which is to come: And hath put all things under His feet, and gave Him to be the head over all things to the church (Ephesians 1:21-22).

Praise God! Jesus has been given the name that is above every other name!

That at the name of Jesus every knee should bow, of things in heaven, and things in earth, and things under the earth; and that every tongue should confess that Jesus Christ is Lord, to the glory of God the Father (Philippians 2:10-11).

All things are in subjection to Him. Everything in Heaven, on earth, and beneath the earth must obey Him.

Now, are you ready for this?

All that Jesus is and all of the power and authority that He possesses is in His name!

All of the fullness of the Godhead is in His name.

Salvation, healing, creative power, deliverance, and everything you may need is in His name!

When you call upon the name of Jesus, you invoke—put into operation—the power and authority that is in that name to manifest the healing, deliverance, or whatever you need.

Christ Manifests Himself Through His Name

When you speak Jesus' name in faith, He is there. He manifests Himself through His name.

In Matthew 18:20, Jesus revealed the secret of why two or more can agree and receive what they ask for. He said: *"For where two or three are gathered together in My name, there am I in the midst of them."*

He wasn't talking about when two or more are gathered together in a church service. In essence, Jesus was saying that whenever two or more believers gather together in the power and authority of His name and agree, He is there!

Whenever you need to exercise the authority that Jesus has given to you over sickness or any other attack of the enemy, find another Spirit-filled believer, and agree with them in the name of Jesus. Whatever you ask for will be done because Jesus is there with you, at that moment, to meet your need.

Satan Has Been Operating Illegally

Jesus defeated and stripped satan of his power over us. The Church—you and I—have been given power over all of the power of the enemy. Yet, because we have failed to exercise the authority that belongs to us in Jesus' name, satan has continued to attack us with every form of sickness and disease.

When satan tries to bring sickness on your body, he is doing it illegally. You have been delivered out of his dominion. Immediately, when satan hits you with symptoms of sickness, don't run to the medicine cabinet. Take authority over him and the sickness.

In the name of Jesus, command the symptoms to leave. When you use the name of Jesus, remember that all that He is and all of the power He has today is in His name. Then, receive your healing, in faith. Put your faith into action. Trust God to manifest the healing in your body.

God has not planned for you to be defeated! Jesus has given you His name. Now, by faith, I want you to stretch your hand toward Heaven, and take possession of that name. Reach your hand up to Him right now. You have known about the power that was in His name.

You may have used His name in prayer. Right now, I want you to receive a fresh revelation of the power that is behind His name. Take full possession of it!

———◄o►———

Make the Following the Prayer of Your Heart Today:

Dear Jesus, by faith, I reach out and take full possession of the power and authority that You have given to me in Your name. Thank You for the name that is above every name. From this day forward, I will exercise the legal right to use Your name. I take authority now, in Your mighty name, over every sickness and disease that is afflicting my body. I command it to go now. I receive my healing now and praise You for it!

Strategy #6: Accept and Claim Your Healing By Faith

Scripture Reading: Mark 10:46-52, John 9:1-7, and Luke 17:10-19

Don't ever accept your sickness or disease or resign yourself to it. Never think that there is nothing that can be done or that you will have to learn to live with your condition!

Take hold of God's contract for your healing even before you see a physical manifestation of it. Accept your healing. Do not accept it based on how you feel or according to your physical condition but according to the promises that are in God's contract of healing.

Christ Always Responds to the Cry of Faith

In Mark chapter 10, we read that when blind Bartimaeus heard that Jesus was passing by, he refused to be denied. He refused to accept the fact that he would remain a blind beggar until the day he died. He was sitting along the side of the road begging when he heard the noise and excitement of the people rushing past him. When he learned that Jesus was passing by, he cried out in a loud voice: *"Jesus, Thou Son of David, have mercy on me"* (Mark 10:47).

The people tried to stop him, but he could not be silenced! In desperation, he cried even louder, at the top of his voice: *"Thou son of David, have mercy on me"* (Mark 10:48).

Above the noise of the crowd, Jesus heard his cry of faith and stood still.

He asked for Bartimaeus to be brought to Him.

Bartimaeus's faith grew stronger. He rose to his feet, cast aside his beggar's garment, and made his way to Jesus. He knew that if he could just get to Jesus, he would be healed.

Bartimaeus Received Because He Dared to Act in Faith

Jesus asked him: *"What do you want Me to do for you?"* (Mark 10:51 NIV). It was obvious that Bartimaeus was blind, but Jesus was testing his faith. Bartimaeus replied: *"Lord, that I might receive my sight"* (Mark 10:51).

In response to Bartimaeus's faith, Jesus spoke the Word of healing: *"Go thy way; thy faith hath made thee whole"* (Mark 10:52). As Jesus spoke, the healing power of Almighty God was released into Bartimaeus's eyes. Immediately, his blind eyes were opened.

Bartimaeus received his sight because he dared to act in faith and press his way through to Jesus. In every example of healing that God has given to us in His Word, it was the act or expression of faith that enabled the individual to receive the miracle of healing that they needed.

Dare to Believe, and Act in Faith and Obedience to God's Word

On another occasion, when Jesus was in Jerusalem, He healed a man who had been blind from birth. He spat on the ground, mixed the spittle with dirt, formed it into a ball of clay, anointed the man's eyes with it, and told him to go wash in the pool of Siloam.

There was no healing virtue in the spit or in the clay. There was no healing power in the water in the pool of Siloam. Jesus used these methods to cause the man to exercise his faith. The man went to the pool of Siloam blind and came from it seeing *because he dared to believe and act in faith and obedience* to Christ.

It wasn't the method He used that healed him. It was according to the man's faith! If he had failed to act in faith and obedience to Christ's command to wash in the pool of Siloam, he would never have received his healing.

Act in Faith Before Your Healing Is Manifested

Ten lepers were healed when they acted in faith upon the Word of healing that Christ had spoken to them. *"And as He entered into a certain village, there met Him ten men that were lepers, which stood afar off"* (Luke 17:12). Because of their unclean condition, they did not come near to Jesus. They stood at a distance. They had not resigned themselves to remain in their condition (with the loathsome leprosy eating away their flesh) but came near enough to where Jesus was passing by. When they recognized who He was, they cried out for mercy: *"Jesus, Master, have mercy on us"* (Luke 17:13).

Jesus heard their cry of faith. When He saw them, He told them: *"Go shew yourselves unto the priests..."*

(Luke 17:14). He could have just spoken a Word, and the dreaded leprosy would have instantly disappeared. He could have laid hands on them and healed them there, but He didn't. Instead, Jesus required them to act on their faith.

Their condition was unchanged. The dreaded leprosy was still there, but Jesus told them to show themselves to the priests and have them tested to see that they had been healed. The Word says that as they went—as they acted in faith on Christ's Word to them—they were healed! *"And it came to pass, that, as they went, they were cleansed"* (Luke 17:14).

Only one of the ten lepers returned to give thanks. One of the lepers (a Samaritan), after recognizing that he had been healed, came running back to Jesus. He fell at Jesus' feet and praised and glorified God. After asking about the remaining nine lepers who had been healed, Jesus said to him: *"Arise, go thy way: thy faith hath made thee whole"* (Luke 17:19).

Faith Has Substance. It Sustains, Strengthens, and Upholds You!

Jesus used many different methods to heal. The important thing was not the method that He used but the response of faith of the person. Faith enables you to take possession of all that Christ has provided for you through His death and resurrection. The saving of your soul, delivering of your spirit, supernaturally providing for your physical needs, and divine healing are released in response to your faith!

Apostle Paul gives a clear understanding of what real faith is in Hebrews 11:1: *"Now faith is the substance of things hoped for, the evidence of things not seen."* Faith is a substance. It is not wishful thinking, not just hoping, not a mental belief, but something substantial that sustains, strengthens, and upholds you.

The word *substance* in this verse means, "the ground upon which one builds a hope." It is translated from the Greek word, *hupostasis. Stasis* means "to stand." *Hupo* means "under."[1] Apostle Paul was saying that faith is the substance (the foundation, the ground) upon which we build our hope.

The supernatural faith of God is a strong foundation upon which you firmly stand, rooted and grounded. It is by this faith that you are able to stand firm to believe God for your healing, regardless of the circumstances, pain, or discouragement that you may face.

Faith Grabs Hold of Things That Are Unseen and Counts Them As Fact

The writer of Hebrews said: *"Faith is...the evidence of things not seen"* (Heb. 11:1). The word *evidence,* when translated from the original Greek, means "proof" and "conviction."[2] Faith is the proof of the things you desire from God that you do not see (the healing you need in your body) and a strong, firm conviction of their reality.

Faith grabs hold of the things that you do not see and that are not revealed to your natural senses and counts them as a fact—a living reality.

Faith rests upon fact! It is settled in your mind. There is no doubt, no striving. You rest in the fact that *it will* come to pass!

Faith Moves You From the Natural to the Supernatural

Faith acts upon fact! When you know that you have already received the healing that you have asked God in prayer for, you must put your faith into action. If you are believing God for a healing in your body, do something that you were unable to do before. Believe that you have received your healing. Whatever your need may be, act in faith (as if you have already received it), before you see a manifestation of it!

Faith upholds fact! Faith becomes a strong foundation underneath you that enables you to keep believing, regardless of what your five senses may otherwise reveal. It takes you out of the natural realm and into the spiritual realm. It takes you into a new dimension. You will be able to see, by the Spirit, the things that you need as having become a reality, regardless of all of the things that would contradict it or say it is not possible.

Refuse to Be Moved by What You Think, See, or Feel!

After you pray, you may not see or feel any change in your physical condition. Your symptoms may increase, or your condition may grow worse. You must not be moved by what you see, what you think, or how you feel. *"For we walk by faith, not by sight"* (2 Cor. 5:7).

T.L. Osborn, in his book, *Healing the Sick*, says concerning praying and standing in faith:

> *Praying the prayer of faith does not necessarily mean that the answer is seen or felt immediately. Whether it is done instantly or by a gradual healing does not matter. His Word stands true, and it is for us to believe and doubt not, trusting Him to completely and thoroughly take away the disease.*[3]

There are many people who believe the Word and accept their healing as long as they can see a manifestation of their healing. However, as soon as symptoms appear, or they feel pain, their faith wavers. They cast out the Word and stop believing and confessing God's promises of healing. They start confessing their sickness and talking about their symptoms, which annuls their prayer of faith.

Act in Faith, and Receive Your Healing Now!

Friend, the work has been done! Everything that is necessary for the manifestation of the healing you need in your body (or in the body of one of your loved ones) has already been accomplished!

It's up to you now to respond. Act in faith upon the Word that God has already spoken. All that is necessary is for you to cry in faith, as blind Bartimaeus did: "Jesus, Thou Son of David, have mercy on me! Heal me!"

When Bartimaeus cried in faith to Jesus, Christ heard him through the crowd and stood still. Then, He had Bartimaeus brought to Him.

Anywhere, at any time, and in any place that you cry out to Christ, in faith, He will heal you! He is ready and willing to heal you now, as you release your faith.

Make the Following a Statement of Your Faith:

I take hold of God's contract of healing! According to Isaiah 53:5 and First Peter 2:24, by the stripes that Jesus took on His back, **I am healed!** *I believe that He took my sicknesses, diseases, and infirmities upon Himself. Since He carried them for me, I don't have to carry them. By faith, I receive my healing now. I put my faith into action and will continue to believe and confess God's promises until I receive the full manifestation of my healing.*

Endnotes

1. http://www.searchgodsword.org.

2. Ibid.

3. T.L. Osborn, *Healing the Sick* (Osborn International, 1992).

Day 21

STRATEGY #7: PRAISE AND WORSHIP GOD IN ADVANCE FOR YOUR TOTAL HEALING

Scripture Reading: Second Chronicles 20:1-30 and Acts 16:16-40

As you release faith for your healing, one of the most important keys is to praise and worship God. Thank Him *in advance* for healing your body.

Praise sets your victory in motion!

Something supernatural happens when you begin to sing, praise, and worship God. There is a release in the spirit and new freedom. The enemy of your soul cannot stand! As the joy of the Lord and songs of praise rise up out of your heart unto the Lord, satan knows that he is defeated and must retreat.

Praise Enables You to Keep Your Focus on God and His Power

In Second Chronicles chapter 20, we read the familiar story of Jehoshaphat and the children of Israel. They were facing their enemies, and they were greatly outnumbered. When Jehoshaphat heard the news that the great multitude of the armies of the Ammonites, Moabites, and their allied forces were coming to battle against them, his heart was filled with fear. However, the first thing he did was to proclaim a fast throughout all of Judah.

Jehoshaphat pleaded their case before the Lord and acknowledged their inabilities and total dependence upon Him to deliver them out of the hands of their enemies. He told God: *"We have no might against this great company that cometh against us; neither know we what to do: but our eyes are upon Thee"* (2 Chron. 20:12).

When you feel the onslaught of the enemy (his attacks against your physical body), it is not easy to keep your spiritual focus upon God. Many times, you may be so overwhelmed that you keep your eyes focused upon your circumstances, instead of keeping them focused upon God and the assurance that He will heal you.

Praise Set Their Miracle in Motion!

Notice the battle strategy that Jehoshaphat and the children of Israel used. Jehoshaphat appointed singers to go before the army to sing praises to the Lord. Their strength wasn't in their own abilities. Their faith and confidence was in Almighty God. When they began to release praises unto God, it set their miracle in motion!

> *And when they began to sing and to praise, the Lord set ambushments against the children of Ammon, Moab, and mount Seir, which were come against Judah; and they were smitten* (2 Chronicles 20:22).

It wasn't necessary for the army of Judah to even lift their swords! God fought for them. He brought confusion into their enemies' camp and delivered them into their hands. It took them three days to gather the spoils of the battle!

Their praises ascended before God and brought down His power to deliver them. God gave them total victory over their enemies!

Release Praises Unto God, Even Before You See an Outward Manifestation of Your Healing!

You may be facing circumstances in your life that seem impossible in the natural. You may be suffering from a longstanding sickness or disease. You may be weary of the battle. Like the children of Israel, you may feel trapped. The enemy may be coming against you with full force.

Don't stop where you are. Don't stop believing and trusting God to bring you His healing and deliverance!

Go forward! Face your circumstances. Begin to sing the praises of God. Thank and praise Him for His mighty, healing power and for healing your body.

You may be thinking, I don't feel like singing a song of victory and praise to the Lord. How can I possibly sing when I am in pain, and my body is still afflicted with sickness and disease?

You can sing His praises and worship Him even *before* you receive the full manifestation of your healing because He is your God. He is *Jehovah-rapha*, the God who heals you! Your victory is not dependent upon your circumstances. It is dependent upon knowing God—not as a powerful force, somewhere far removed in the heavens—intimately. Knowing that He has provided healing for your body in the Atonement, begin to rejoice, and sing His praises.

Praise Delivered Paul and Silas Out of Prison

Praise was the powerful weapon that brought Paul and Silas deliverance from prison. They had been beaten and thrown into a dark, rat-infested jail cell. Their feet were in stocks. Blood poured out of the wounds on their backs where the soldiers had beaten them. They were exhausted, and their backs throbbed with pain.

Instead of letting words of defeat and discouragement come out of their mouths, they began to lift their voices. They started to sing praises unto God. I imagine that as they sang, their voices grew stronger and stronger and louder and louder, until all of the prisoners heard them. Paul and Silas weren't having a pity party. They weren't grumbling and complaining about the treatment that they had received from the soldiers. Neither were they binding the devil or crying out for God to deliver them.

Their deliverance came as they sang praises to God! Their praise and worship set their miracle in motion! As they sang, the walls of their cell began to shake violently. God heard their praises and supernaturally intervened. He shook the prison, until the entire foundation was shaken. All of the doors of the prison cells flew open, and all of the shackles were loosed from the prisoners.

Praise Is a Powerful Weapon That Defeats the Enemy!

God inhabits the praises of His people! When you begin to praise and worship God, satan must retreat! Satan knows that when your heart is focused on God, and you are pouring your worship upon Him, your faith is being released. Your praise draws a response from God. His presence is manifested, and sickness and disease cannot remain! The powers of darkness that are afflicting your body must go!

David knew the power of praise. He praised God seven times a day (see Ps. 119:164.) He said, *"I will bless the Lord at all times: His praise shall continually be in my mouth"* (Ps. 34:1). Praise was a mighty weapon in his mouth. He also said, *"Let the high praises of God be in their mouth, and a two-edged sword in their hand"* (Ps. 149:6); and, *"I will call upon the Lord, who is worthy to be praised: so shall I be saved from mine enemies"* (Ps. 18:3). David called upon the Lord with praise because he knew that God was worthy of all praise. As a result of his praise, David was saved from his enemies.

Offer Up Praises to God Continually!

Instead of worrying or becoming fearful, begin to praise God!

Instead of complaining and murmuring about your physical disabilities, release praise to God!

Instead of focusing on your symptoms or talking about your sickness, sing praises to God!

As you offer up to God sacrifices of praise (even when you face desperate circumstances), God will honor that praise with answered prayer!

Have a continual praise in your heart and upon your lips. During your time alone with God, spend time first just praising and thanking Him for all that He has done for you and for releasing His healing power into your body. Paul said:

> *Be careful for nothing; but in every thing by prayer and supplication with thanksgiving let your requests be made known unto God. And the peace of God, which passeth all understanding, shall keep your hearts and minds through Christ Jesus* (Philippians 4:6-7).

Paul said that we are to present all of our requests *with thanksgiving*!

Live in an Atmosphere of Praise and Worship

Fill your home with worship music. Throughout the day, stop frequently to praise God for your healing. Don't wait until you see an outward manifestation. Offer up praises to God, and know that He has heard you. By His stripes, you are healed.

As you drive to work, worship and praise God for His mighty power and love toward you. Pour out your love upon Him. As you go about your work, wherever you are, take time to release praises to God. Take every possible opportunity to testify to family members, friends, co-workers, and neighbors of God's healing power.

Friend, take hold of God's contract of healing today. Begin to praise Him with all that is within you. Use these seven strategies to break every bondage of sickness and disease that may be afflicting your body. God wants you to be healed and to walk and live in divine health!

—————◄○►—————

Make This Declaration of Your Faith:

Praise is a powerful weapon that defeats the enemy. As I release praises to God, it will set my miracle in motion! Like David, I will praise the Lord at all times. His praise will continually be in my mouth. I praise Him now for healing me and removing sickness and disease from me. I will offer up sacrifices of praise, knowing that He has heard me. He will make me victorious over all of the power of the enemy.

About the Ministry of Dr. Morris Cerullo
President of Morris Cerullo World Evangelism

Morris Cerullo's accreditation for ministry is, in itself, quite formidable: a divine, supernatural call from God to preach and evangelize when he was only 15 years old, and over half a century of experience as a pastor, teacher, author of more than 200 books, and worldwide evangelist.

Many honors have been bestowed on Morris Cerullo, including honorary Doctorates of Divinity and Humanities, by academic and spiritual leaders and heads of state around the world in recognition of his achievements and contributions to global evangelization.

Dr. Cerullo is respected and revered by millions around the world, including over one and a half million Nationals who have been trained through Morris Cerullo's Schools of Ministry. His ministry outreaches include:

> **The Morris Cerullo *Helpline* Program**—a major television cable and satellite weekly, hour-long, Prime Time broadcast that reaches out to hurting people in virtually every nation on earth.

> **Schools of Ministry**—training national pastors, ministers, and laypeople to reach their nations for Christ through mass evangelistic crusades.

Mission to All the World—reaching the entire world, region by region, with Schools of Ministry, miracle crusades, television Prime Time specials, and local Schools of Ministry that are designed to cover every village, city, and town in every region.

Victory! **Television**—cutting-edge, daily television programming that is designed to strengthen the Body of Christ to reach the entire world.

Dr. Cerullo has made a tremendous impact on the destiny of the nations of the world.

He has sacrificially dedicated his life to helping hurting people and equipping others who will take the message that has been given to them and train others.

WE CARE

Brother and Sister Cerullo,

please place these requests on the miracle prayer
altar, and pray for these needs:

_____

_____

_____

_____

_____

_____

_____

_____

_____

_____

❏ Enclosed is my love gift of $_____to help you win souls and support this worldwide ministry.

❏ Please tell me how I can become a God's Victorious Army member to help you to reach the nations of the world and to receive more anointed teachings on a monthly basis!

Name:_____

Address:_____

City:_____State/_____

Prov:_____

Zip/Postal Code:_____

Phone Number: (_____) _____

E-mail:_____

Mail today to:

Morris Cerullo World Evangelism
P.O. Box 85277 • San Diego, CA 92186-5277

Morris Cerullo World Evangelism
P.O. Box 3600 • Concord, Ontario L4K 1B6

Morris Cerullo World Evangelism
P.O. Box 277 • Hemel Hempstead, Herts HP2 7DH

DESTINY IMAGE PUBLISHERS, INC.

*"Speaking to the Purposes of God for This Generation
and for the Generations to Come."*

VISIT OUR NEW SITE HOME AT
WWW.DESTINYIMAGE.COM

FREE SUBSCRIPTION TO DI NEWSLETTER

Receive free unpublished articles by top DI authors, exclusive

discounts, and free downloads from our best and newest books.

Visit www.destinyimage.com to subscribe.

Write to: Destiny Image
                P.O. Box 310
                Shippensburg, PA 17257-0310

Call: 1-800-722-6774

Email: orders@destinyimage.com

For a complete list of our titles or to place an order
online, visit www.destinyimage.com.

FIND US ON FACEBOOK OR FOLLOW US ON TWITTER.

www.facebook.com/destinyimage   facebook
www.twitter.com/destinyimage   twitter